Applying Project Management in the Workplace

Revised Edition

Applying Project Management in the Workplace

Revised Edition

Jeff Crow

Blackbird Publishing
Portland, Oregon

Library of Congress Catalog Card Number: 97-80355

Applying Project Management in the Workplace

© Copyright, 1997, 1999, Jeff D. Crow
All rights reserved.

ISBN: 0-9660469-1-9

Printed in the United States of America

Blackbird Publishing
PO Box 80746
Portland, OR 97280-1746
1-888-674-0010

*With heartfelt thanks to all the students
and workshop participants who, over the years,
have contributed so much to the content,
organization, and presentation of this book
and to my own understanding of
project management inside organizations.*

Applying Project Management in the Workplace

Table of Contents

**Chapter 7
Checklists and Form
Masters**

Checklists:

Forms:

Appendices

**Appendix A: A Problem-Solving
Process**

**Appendix B: Problem-Solving
Tools:**

Chapter 1
Introduction

1

Introduction

Welcome

This book is the result of many years of research into the available information on project management and experimentation with the various concepts, tools and techniques I've found. The basic text was created for a specific client with a specific problem in about 1985. Since then, it has undergone countless revisions and updates.

What you hold here is the culmination of a search for tools and techniques that work in the internal business environment. In the years I have been a project manager and have taught project management, both in the university and community college arenas and in numerous public and private sector organizations, one thing has become glaringly obvious:

> Employees working on projects inside organizations need simple, portable, flexible tools to plan and manage their projects in order to succeed.

The concepts, tools and techniques in this book are aimed at addressing the particular needs of employees working on projects developed by, or assigned to them as part of their work. I have tried to include more tools than any one project manager would ordinarily need with the intention that the reader try several options and choose and adapt those that work best in their individual circumstances.

I am constantly seeking to improve and expand the information in this book. Most of the revisions in this edition are from students in my workshops and others in the project management field. I encourage you to contact me with your comments and suggestions. I can be reached at:

Crow Development Corporation
PO Box 80746
Portland, OR 97280-1746
E-mail: jcrow@crowdevelopment.com

Project Management Defined

66 99

If they buy the premise, they'll buy
the joke.

Johnny Carson
Former Tonight Show Host

For those who want a formal definition of Project Management, this is
the one used in this book:

> Project Management is the process by which actions are planned,
> resources organized, and activities initiated and managed to
> achieve a specific goal or purpose, or to produce a specified deliv-
> erable.

This text presents an approach to project management that is some
what different from those commonly used. The difference centers
around a basic assumption about how projects are handled by employees within existing organizations:

> The project manager within an organization is rarely a manager in
> a traditional sense.

Frequently, individuals are given responsibility for a project based on
their expertise in the area that the project impacts. For example, a
technically-oriented individual may be given responsibility for a development project based solely on his or her perceived expertise in that
technology — not on their management ability, position in the organization, or experience. Project managers in organizations are almost always expected to be active participants in the work of their projects
— they are not expected (or even allowed) to be "managers" in the
traditional sense. A more appropriate title would be "project leader."

This unique characteristic of projects undertaken within organizations
creates some problems with the generally accepted approaches to
project management. Since project leaders within organizations are
frequently not in management positions. They do not have the traditional hierarchy behind them. They do not have common managerial
responsibilities or authority such as "hire-and-fire" authority; responsibility for employee performance reviews; the power to grant raises or
promotions; disciplinary authority; etc. Even those who are managers
frequently must work their projects with personnel who do not report
to them. The problems this situation can create are not usually addressed by project management methodologies which assume true
managerial authority and responsibility as a prerequisite for undertaking a project.

This text addresses the lack of managerial authority in several ways:

- There is an emphasis on negotiation. This is a skill which will allow a project leader to develop a team and the technical and support assistance necessary to successfully complete a project
  without relying on non-existent authority.

- There is a section dealing specifically with leadership with an emphasis on leading project teams. There is also a section on the origins and use of power and authority within organizations that provides insights into how truly effective project leaders achieve goals and gather support without relying on "position power" (power granted by one's position within the hierarchy of the organization).

- There is extensive material on developing and working with teams made up of individuals who are not dedicated to the project on a full-time basis.

- Most of the tools, techniques and forms described in this text are designed for non-managers.

The Structure of the Text

For the most part, this text is organized to follow the way most projects unfold. It begins with this introductory section which is devoted to some basic concepts about projects and project management. This is followed by sections covering project pre-work and preliminary planning; project teams and people skills; project planning; project implementation; and finally, the transfer of project output and close-out of the project. Two reference sections finish out the book: A collection of project-related checklists and copy masters of forms described in the text from which project leaders can select the ones most appropriate for their projects and their leadership style; and a series of Appendices of useful project planning, management and problem-solving tools.

At the end of chapters 1, 2, 4, 5, and 6, information has been included under the heading "Issues by Project Type." This information is based on the concept that most projects fall into one of three broad categories:

- Projects to develop or enhance processes for doing work within the organization.

- Projects to develop or enhance the products or services of the organization that are offered to the organization's customers.

- Projects to develop software for either internal use or external sale.

As mentioned earlier, this book is organized to parallel how most projects unfold. This information is intended to call attention to issues of special concern when dealing with each type of project related to the material covered in the chapter. Chapter 3: **People Skills for Project Leaders** is the exception to this as the material in this chapter applies and is useful throughout the life of a project.

Most of the chapters contain descriptions of specific techniques and examples of tools that can be used to plan or manage the issues being discussed. Chapter 7: **Checklists and Form Masters** contains master copies of each of the tools included in the text as well as some additional tools and descriptions of techniques not discussed in the text. Since the "one-size-fits-all" approach almost never works in practice, tools and techniques in a wide range of "sizes" have been included. Try them on and see what "fits."

This book is designed to provide a reference and resource manual for project leaders. Not all concepts apply to all projects. Not all tools are appropriate for every project leader. Not all techniques will work in every case. Examine the concepts in light of what you know about your own situation and work environment. Try the tools and techniques that appeal to you. Adopt and adapt those that work.

Good luck on your projects.

Why Projects?

Organizations undertake projects for a variety of reasons. One of the most common is to allow the organization to do something it has never done before. The degree of uniqueness varies greatly from organization to organization but, overall, projects are undertaken to do something that can't be done within the normal operating systems of the business.

Most organizations place a high value on predictability. The organizational operating systems are in place for the expressed purpose of controlling activities and predicting what will happen in both the short-term and the long-term. Accounting systems are set up to track and detail the use of the organization's financial resources. Production control systems are in use to predict, monitor and control the manufacturing capabilities of the business. Even marketing forecasting systems are intended to predict demand for the company's products or services.

Innovation is, by its very nature, unpredictable. It does not respond to the same controls as on-going operations. And, very definitely, projects in most of their guises are forms of innovation.

Projects are commonly undertaken to develop a new product; improve or develop a process; write a piece of software; enhance a method of accomplishing work; or to accomplish any of a thousand other objectives. Whatever the reason, it is likely that the normal systems of the business would demand more predictability and require more control than can reasonably be expected when doing something new.

The controls and systems of established businesses are very good at doing things millions of times with great reliability. They are not good at doing things for the first time. This is where projects come in. And, as mentioned in the Introduction, project leaders within organizations rarely have the full scope of managerial authority the title implies. Working within these constraints is the subject of this text.

The establishment of the project's goal is the first step in actually planning the project. Without a clear, concise goal statement, most projects flounder. The goal sets the expectations of the project team, the project's sponsors and the project's customers. A process for developing the project goal is discussed in the next chapter.

The Involvement of Several People
" "

Fortunately, it appears that most people are more cooperative than the standard economic model suggests.
Richard Thaler
Cornell University

For most projects undertaken within organizations, the project teams are made up of individuals who are not assigned to the project full time. In most organizations, projects are conducted in parallel with on-going operations. They operate within the confines of the business, use the resources of the business and, are in constant contact with the business. But, they are not managed in the same fashion as the rest of the business. This characteristic places some unique demands on the project leader. Unless the business is a true "matrix organization," the chances are quite good that most of the members of the project team will report (organizationally) to someone other than the project leader. The specific issues this type of organization raises will be discussed in some detail later in this book.

At this point, we should say that virtually all of the people assigned to a project should be thought of as "borrowed resources." This means, they can be called away from the project whenever there is need for their services elsewhere.

Limited Resources
" "

You never know what you can do without until you try.
Franklin Pierce Adams
1881-1960
American Journalist

In even the most research-and-development-driven organizations, there are limits on resources. For the types of projects that will be discussed here, these limits are very tight. They include *all* resources: Time, people, money, materials, space, etc. Sometimes the resource limits are flexible enough, or broad enough, to allow project activity to go on without much concern for reaching limits. However, in most cases, the limits placed on resources are a major determining factor in what can be done on the project.

A Sequencing of Activities
" "

In every affair consider what precedes and what follows, and then undertake it.
Epictetus
circa 60
Greek Philosopher

Some things must be completed before other things can begin. Some things can be done together. Some things can be done completely separately. But, in all cases, there is a sequence to activities which places some constraints on project activity. This sequencing of activities is one of the things that makes project planning possible and project planning is a *major* part of project management.

The "Triple Constraint"

" "

Quality. Speed. Price. Pick two.
Advertising agency lobby sign

All projects, regardless of size or complexity, are bounded by a "Triple Constraint" of time, resources, and output.

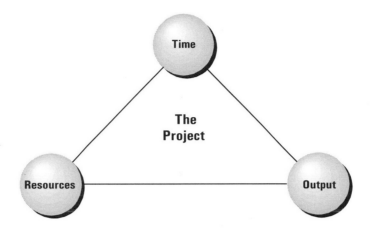

The triple constraint is usually visualized as a triangle with each constraint placed at a corner of the triangle. The area of the triangle is the "space" within which the project must be done.

Time

The Time constraint encompasses all of the time limitations on the project: When it must be delivered, the time demands on the people who must be involved, the time demands on the equipment that must be used, the time constraints placed on the project by management, etc. Of all of the constraints placed on projects, the deadline for delivery is usually the least flexible. This does not, however, mean that the way in which the time from the initiation of the project to the deadline is used is also inflexible. On most projects, the amount of time that can be devoted to the work is flexible, based on the importance the organization places on completion of the project.

Resources

The Resource constraint encompasses all the limitations placed on the project that involve either money or the things money can buy: Material, outside expertise, machinery and equipment, space, and most of all, the time and expertise of the members of the project team.

If you think of resources as the "currency" you can spend to accomplish your project, then the most common denomination of that currency will be other people's time. Most project leaders in businesses today do not control the budgets for their projects. In many cases, they don't even know what the financial constraints are. Likewise, they do not usually have control over the things that money buys such as outside experts, equipment, raw materials and space. This doesn't mean project leaders can't influence these expenditures. However, they don't usually have direct authority over them.

Output

The Output constraint encompasses all the requirements placed on the final output of the project. This includes the performance and quality characteristics: What it must be able to do when it is delivered.

Of all the constraints placed on projects, this is generally the most difficult to define clearly at the outset. This is not to say that it is impossible, but it will require work and negotiation to insure that the deliverable at the end meets the expectations set at the beginning.

The Impact of Changing a Constraint " "

Certainty generally is illusion, and repose is not the destiny of man.
Oliver Wendell Holmes, Jr.
1841-1935
U.S. Supreme Court Justice

As long as the constraints remain stable, all is well. However, stability is not common on projects. During most projects, one or more of the constraints originally set will change. As the illustrations on the following pages show, moving one of the corners of the triangle changes the size and shape of the project's "space." In order to complete the project, changes may be required in the other two constraints.

Unfortunately, constraints rarely get changed in a positive direction. It is rare to get more time, more resources or reduced output requirements. The opposite is generally the case. Most projects are planned and scheduled to deliver the originally specified output within a fairly tight schedule and with very limited flexibility in resources. So, if one or more of the constraints tightens, the others must "pick up the slack."

The trap inherent in this situation lies in not acknowledging that the change in one constraint has made an impact on the other constraints on the project. A change in a constraint requires decisions and actions to keep the project viable.
Examples of the impact of changing a constraint might be:

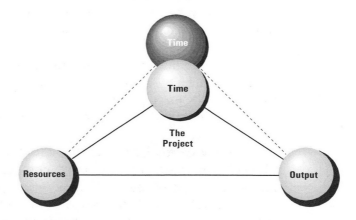

- Changing the time constraint (which usually means shortening the timeline for the project) will require one of two actions:

  - More resources will be required to meet the output requirements for the project, or

- The requirements for the output will need to be adjusted to compensate for the reduced time available to deliver.

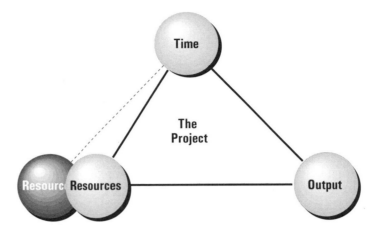

- Changing the resource constraint (which usually means losing resources, either people or money) will require:

  - More time to meet the output requirements, or

  - Adjusting the output requirements to compensate for the lack of resources.

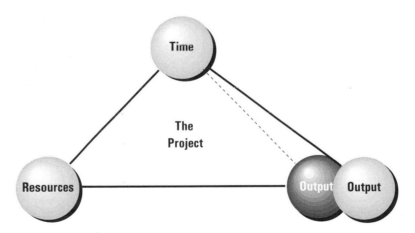

- Changing the output constraint (which usually means adding functions or capabilities to the project's output) will require:

  - More time to develop, test and add the new functions, or

  - Increasing the resources (people and/or money) to compensate for the additional work.

"Tradeoff" is the name of the game. There are tradeoffs inherent in virtually every change in a project. Being able to negotiate these tradeoffs is one of the marks of a good project leader. It is also a major responsibility.

The Characteristics of Effective Project Leaders

Like projects, effective project leaders share some specific characteristics. Effective project leaders are:

- "People" people.

- Good planners.

- Good problem-solvers.

- Goal-driven.

- Action-oriented.

- "Business-aware."

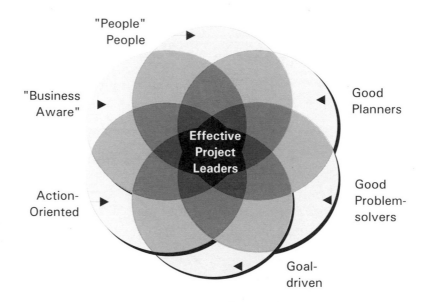

"People" People

Plans do not accomplish project goals. Schedules do not deliver project output. Monitoring systems do not get anything done. Project management software does not manage projects. People are required for every activity connected with a project. People do the work, accomplish the goals, deliver the results, monitor the progress, manage the activities.

In order to be an effective project leader, you must first be an effective "people" person. This does not necessarily mean you must have experience as a people manager. It does mean you must have the ability to be, or to become, an effective leader of people.

Most successful project leaders do not rely on organizational authority (the authority which comes with positions or titles). They rely on their own personal power to motivate and inspire.

Another dimension of being a "people" person is respect. I know of at least one very successful project leader who has been overheard making the following statement more than once:

> "I assume every person I meet and work with on a project is a genius. I assume that they are on my project because they can do things that neither I, nor any other person on the team can do. I try to make this clear to them from our first meeting and this is the way I treat them until they prove me wrong. And, you know what? I'm rarely proven wrong."

Being an effective "people" person does not mean spending all your time making sure everyone is happy. It means treating people with respect; respect for them as individuals; as intelligent, competent, valuable members of the team. If you really don't like people and have no respect for what someone else can do or contribute, find something else to do. Project management is not for you.

Good Planners

" "

The will to win is important, but the will to plan is vital.

Joe Paterno
College Football Coach

The bulk of a project leader's job revolves around planning (and replanning). Logic skills, problem-analysis skills, a "big-picture" view — all are manifestations of good planning skills. In addition, good communication skills are needed to convey the details and requirements of project plans to those who must implement them.

Good planners have a methodology they use to do their planning. As you gain experience with planning and managing projects, your own personal planning methodology will evolve. It may be highly complex and detailed or it may be loose and flexible. Whatever the methodology, it should be applied with the same rigor to each and every project you undertake.

Effective project leaders walk a thin line between the macro and micro activities of a project. One of the most dangerous traps a project leader can fall into is that of becoming too involved in the details of some part of the overall project. Good planning and effective monitoring of the plan provide excellent guidelines for when to "get buried in the details" and when to "stick to the big picture."

Good Problem-solvers

" "

Never go out to meet trouble. If you will just sit still, nine cases out of ten, someone will intercept it before it reaches you.

Calvin Coolidge
1872-1933
30th
President of the United States

Effective project leaders get problems solved. They do not necessarily solve every problem that comes along. Rather, they empower members of the project team to solve the problems they discover.

To the effective project leader, a problem is a challenge to be met in the most efficient manner possible. They recognize that problems are inevitable and that, in most cases, the person closest to the problem is the person best suited to solve it. Therefore, when someone comes to them and says, "I have a problem," their initial response is not, "Leave it with me and I'll take care of it." Rather, they respond with, "What do you think we should do about it?" In many (if not most) cases, the person bringing the problem to your attention has already thought about it and has probably thought of at least one or two possible solutions.

What they may be asking is not, "Will you solve this problem for me?" but rather, "Which of my solutions should I try first?" In some cases, it's even more basic. They may really be asking, "Do I have your permission to solve this?" When these situations arise, pick a solution or grant permission. There is only one caution that goes with this: Never forget to close the information loop. The last thing you need is to have problems identified and not know whether they have been effectively dealt with or not. Always finish these conversations with something like, "Try this approach and let me know what happens." It is also a good idea to attach a time-frame to the request for a response such as, "And let me know by tomorrow afternoon." Then, follow up to be sure it worked.

Some problems are really the project leader's responsibility. They are outside the bounds of what the team member can do or they require access to resources the team member can't draw on. When appropriate, the leader should take on the problem.

Effective project leaders also recognize that not every problem can be solved by team members or even by themselves. When a problem like this occurs, they will see that the people who must solve the problem are aware of it and will do what is necessary to get the problem solved at whatever level is appropriate. Effective project leaders don't solve every problem, they see to it that the problems get solved.

Goal-Driven

" "

Men, like nails, lose their usefulness when they lose direction and begin to bend.
Walter Savage Landor
1775-1864
English Poet and Writer

Projects are implemented to accomplish some specific goal. The project plan is based on doing the work necessary to deliver the output of the project. Once the planning is done, effective project leaders tend to be very focused on the accomplishment of that goal. They look at every activity and task, every problem, every deliverable in terms of how it will affect the accomplishment of the project goal.

Decisions are made, contingency plans are implemented, work breakdowns are revised in order to more effectively and efficiently accomplish the goal of the project.

This would be easier if project goals would stay put once they are set. In reality, however, they have a nasty tendency to "drift" or get redefined along the way to their accomplishment. In some cases, this is the result of an intentional change in the requirements for the output. In other cases, it is the result of discoveries made as the project unfolds that require a change in one of the constraints.

Regardless of its stability, the project goal is the target at which all work on the project is aimed. Effective project leaders never let that target out of their sight, no matter how it shifts.

Action-oriented

" "

Don't wait for your ship to come in, swim out to it.

Anonymous

While effective project leaders recognize the importance of detailed planning, they also recognize the need to "get it off the drawing board" and get the project underway. Once project planning is complete, everything centers on the implementation and completion of the activities of the project.

Activities are tracked very carefully and decisions are made which will move the project ahead. Problems are addressed as soon as they appear. Resources are allocated where they will do the most good. Contingency plans are implemented without waiting for a situation to reach the crisis stage. All activity is aimed at accomplishing the project goal within the time frame of the project.

Projects develop a kind of internal momentum as they unfold. They usually start slowly, and build in terms of both activity and speed as they develop. Managing this momentum requires careful monitoring of both the work being done and the people doing it.

"Business-aware"

" "

The creative person wants to be a know-it-all. He wants to know about all kinds of things: ancient history, nineteenth-century mathematics, current manufacturing techniques, flower arranging, and hog futures. Because he never knows when these ideas might come together to form a new idea. It may happen six minutes later or six months or six years down the road. But he has faith that it will happen.

Carl Ally
Founder, Ally & Gargano
Advertising

Unless a company has hired people specifically as project managers — with training and experience in managing projects in a variety of disciplines — project leaders are most likely to be individuals who are selected based on some technical expertise deemed necessary to the completion of the project at hand. This has inherent pitfalls.

There is a natural tendency on the part of technically competent people to work within their personal "comfort zone" which may be too deep in the details of the project. That is, after all, where their expertise lies. Effective project leaders, with technical backgrounds, are able to separate their technical expertise from their project leadership duties. They do this by being "business-aware," that is, being constantly aware of the larger context in which the project is being undertaken. They maintain a clear understanding of how the project fits into the context of the entire business, not just the area in which it is being implemented.

Business awareness is difficult to teach and is usually the result of simple curiosity — some individuals are just more interested in "how it all fits together." It is this orientation on the larger context that helps effective project leaders keep their projects in the proper organizational perspective.

There are benefits to developing your business awareness. For one thing, you are likely to be able to find and utilize resources outside your own area if you know what else is going on in the company and who's doing it. For another, if you are aware of the goals and objectives of the organization, you can link your project closely to one or more of those goals and thereby gain additional support for your work.

The linkage or connection between a project goal and some other goal or objective of the organization is a critical source of support in the on-going struggle for resources, assistance, expertise, time and commitment. If you can draw a clear line between the accomplishment of your project's goal and some other goal of the business, your ability to argue effectively for needed resources and support is greatly improved. Obviously, the higher the goal you can connect to, the better for your project. But, even linking it to a simple work-group goal will help. If you can also connect it clearly to a department goal, so much the better. If you can draw that line from project through work group, through department and into the level of divisional, corporate or organizational goals, your chances of getting and maintaining support for your project improve even more.

In fact, if you can't find a clear linkage between your project goal and some other goal of the organization, you should ask yourself why the project is being undertaken. If there is no connection to the expenditure of resources on the project and the furthering or accomplishment of some organizational goal, why should the organization support the project?

Key Players in the World of Projects

There are several individuals and groups who can have a significant interest in you and your projects. Not all projects have highly defined roles but there are aspects of each of these roles on virtually every project:

- The project's sponsor.

- The project's customer.

- Stakeholders and other interested parties.

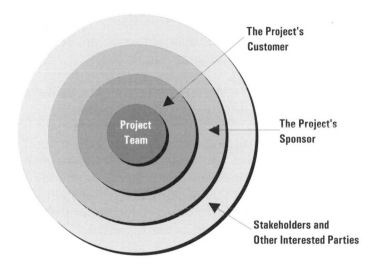

Identifying these players early in the planning process is important to the planning activity. The roles outlined here may be shared by a single person or group or they may be spread among a large number of people and groups. For example, the project's sponsor may also be the project's customer.

Every organization utilizes these roles differently. In some, the roles are clearly defined with a clear set of responsibilities outlined for each. In others, the roles may not even be acknowledged. In all cases, however, these roles exist to some extent.

Project Sponsor

There are two possible definitions for the Sponsor role:

- The person who initiates the project, whether this is the customer or not, and who will be the main source of management decision-making and resource assistance throughout the project.

- A person, usually in management, who will act on behalf of the project when issues exceed the project leader's authority or responsibility. This person may or may not have been the initiator of the project.

Most projects need a sponsor. Due to how project leaders are selected in most organizations, the full range of managerial authority is rarely granted along with the assignment. At some point, outside assistance with decision-making, resource acquisition, or intervention is likely to be needed. Knowing who to go to for this help is important to the continuation and success of the project.

The person in the Sponsor role has certain responsibilities. They should:

• Support the project, the project leader and the project team in their efforts to complete the project successfully.

• They should provide advice and assistance as needed.

• They should act as an advocate for the project, the project leader and project team.

• They should intervene on behalf of the project in situations where outside support is required.

Identifying a Sponsor for your project should be one of the early activities you undertake. In many cases, the Sponsor will be the person who initiated the project, frequently your manager. In those instances where you or someone other than your manager initiate the project, consider who has a vested interest in the success of the project and recruit them as the Sponsor.

Formalizing the Sponsor relationship is not always necessary. However, you should at least have a conversation with your Sponsor to discuss the project and the role you expect them to play in its completion.

Project Customer

A customer is anyone who receives and uses the output of the work you do.

The project's customer is the recipient of the output of the project — the deliverable handed over at the end. Knowing who your customers are is an important key to defining and delivering an output they can use.

In many instances, a project's customers are others inside the organization. They are members of the same work group or a related work group. Or they may be a work group that you and the project team members support in some way as part of your jobs. In these cases, it is easy to speak directly with them and to enlist their input and aid in defining and reviewing the work being done.

Even when the project's customer is outside the organization or otherwise not directly accessible, it is important to consider their needs and situation when developing the project.

With internal customers this is fairly easy — you can go talk to them. With external customers this usually requires either someone who is in contact with them or someone who can effectively represent the customer's interests. Product development projects frequently have representatives from the Marketing or Sales function on the team to act as the customer's stand-in.

Stakeholders and Other Interested Parties

Most projects will touch more than just the project team and the project's customers. Others within the organization will be impacted by either the development of the project or the delivery of the project's output. Identifying who has an interest in your project is an important part of the definition and planning process.

Take, for example, a project to develop a new manufacturing process. The obvious customers for this project are the manufacturing people who will use the new process to do their work. Others who are likely to be impacted by this project include:

- The people who will be responsible for maintaining the process once it is up and running.

- The people in the process that precedes the new process in the manufacturing flow, since the requirements for what they provide may change.

- Production or plant management since they will be responsible for managing the new process.

- Production planning since they will need to plan work for a new process.

- Material control since they will be supplying material to the new process.

- Whomever receives the output of the new manufacturing operation.

Others who could be impacted might include: Design engineering, manufacturing engineering, packaging, shipping, accounting, and marketing.

Projects do not usually come into being in isolation. They are most often initiated to solve an organizational problem. Their output is usually intended to become an integral part of the on-going operation of the business. Identifying who has a stake in your projects will help, both from the point of view of gaining and maintaining support, and from the point of view of creating a project output that has been carefully thought out and can be effectively integrated.

Three Broad Categories of Projects

While the overall flow of project activity is essentially the same regardless of the project being undertaken, there are some unique characteristics which emerge depending on the type of project.

Basically, projects undertaken within a business fall within three broad categories:

- Process projects are usually internally focused on development or enhancement of a process, technique, or method of accomplishing work.

- Product- or service-development projects are usually externally focused on developing and/or providing a product or service to the customers of the business.

- Software development projects can be focused on development of software for internal use or for sale to the company's customers.

Major facilities projects (such as the construction of a new facility, renovation of an existing manufacturing plant or the construction of a retail outlet) are a combination of internally- and externally-focused projects.

Process Projects

The customers of internally-focused process projects are those who will be asked to use the new process once it is developed and implemented. They are your coworkers in the company.

Process projects rarely have huge budgets, are limited in their scope and impact and are usually completed with little involvement of outside vendors (with the exception of those who provide equipment required by the new process).

Internal process projects are by far the most common type of projects undertaken in business today. Much of the driving force for process projects is provided by the need to respond to changes in both the internal and external environments of the business.

Product/Service Projects

The customers of externally-focused product or service development projects are a combination of internal and external: Internal customers are those who will be asked to manufacture the product or provide the service, and external customers are the customers of the company who will purchase the final product or service.

Externally-focused projects tend to receive more attention than internally-focused projects. They tend to have larger budgets and greater access to diverse resources both inside and outside the company. There is usually heavy involvement on the part of the marketing arm of the company and, if carried out in a truly customer-focused manner, a strong dependence on customer input and customer interaction with at least some members of the project team.

Gaining commitment and assistance for an externally-focused project is usually fairly easy due to the fact that these projects are generally intended to generate income and it is easier to show the benefits to the company as a whole.

Software Projects

Software development projects are perhaps the most unique type of project. On most projects, there are physical components that are developed and delivered throughout the life of the project. Even if the project is canceled before completion, there are usually some physical items that show what was done and that can, in some cases, be sold or disposed of by some means to help recover some of the resources expended during the project. (Examples include: Prototype or "first-run" products, land or building materials from a construction project, machinery or equipment from a process project.)

Software is a unique product in that its component parts (the actual lines of computer code) have little, if any, value until they are all integrated into the final program. In fact, they rarely have physical existence as anything other than binary instructions stored on magnetic media. This characteristic makes managing a software development project a unique challenge.

Much of the tracking and monitoring of project activity relies on the delivery of a physical output at various milestones. Software milestones are generally met when certain functions become usable or when a certain proportion of the final code is written. The deliverables of software projects are frequently demonstrations of functionality or printouts of lines of code.

Complex software development projects require extensive focus on the issues surrounding the integration of the component parts of the program into a complete, functional package. They also require careful coordination of technical and non-technical activities (such as the development of documentation to support the software).

Chapter 2
Project Pre-Work

2

Project Pre-Work

Introduction

Before a project can begin, the reason for the project should be clearly understood. Without a clear picture of what needs to be done to meet a specific need, activity is unfocused and generally results in lost time, false starts and confusion.

Project pre-work is a form of problem-solving. In order to solve the problem, you must first define it and clarify what is desired of the solution. In many cases, an uncovered need is the reason why a project is undertaken in the first place. Someone has discovered they need something they don't have. This could come from virtually anywhere inside or outside the organization. Inside the organization, it could be a need for an improved method of working; a new manufacturing technique or process; a new piece of software to automate a task; a consolidation of two or more operations into a single process. From outside the organization it could be a request from a customer for an improvement to an existing product or a request for a new product or service; it could be an idea from an employee for a product or service he or she believes has market potential; it could be an idea seen in a competitor's operation that could be adapted to the organization's needs.

However a project idea originates, simply being aware of the need is not the same thing as really understanding it. Many projects have come into being and lasted for months (or even years) without producing anything significant in the way of output because the exact nature of the need to be addressed has not been clearly understood before project work begins. This is an example of the "Ready! Fire! Aim!" mentality that seems to pervade much of business. The tendency to shoot without aiming is dangerous (and potentially very expensive) if you shoot without clearly understanding what the target is.

At this first stage of the project planning process, several things must be researched to define the need and the response to it:

- The problem to be addressed by the project.

- What to do about it.

- For whom to do it.

- By whom the work should be done.

- By when it must be delivered.

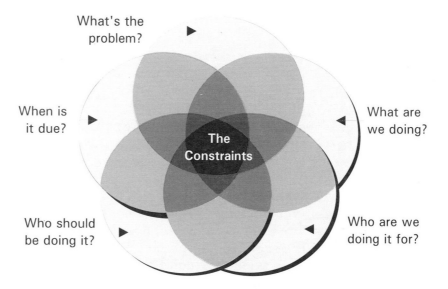

Researching this information will help to define the constraints of:

- Time.

- Resources.

- Output.

In this chapter, you will explore several aspects of project pre-work. You will look at a comprehensive process for developing an understanding of the need for the project and for developing significant information about the best response to that need. You will also examine the importance of having a clear project goal and look at a simple process for developing one. Next, you will be presented with a simple tool for defining the skills needed to do the work of the project and for linking the individuals to those skills. Finally, you will be given some basic things to consider when developing or recruiting the project team.

Researching the Need

" "

A problem well stated is a problem half solved.

Charles F. Kettering
1876-1958
American Electrical Engineer
and Inventor

There are as many ways to research a need as there are unfulfilled needs. What you need to do at this stage is to reach an understanding of each of the issues listed above.

The following process is designed to provide a structure for project pre-work. Some projects are very straight-forward and do not require extensive pre-work analysis. Others are more ill-defined, poorly thought out, or more complex. Yet others have numerous possible solutions or outcomes, any one of which might solve the problem. This pre-work process will guide you through defining the problem and some of the requirements of any solution to it; developing options and alternatives; analyzing which option will best solve the problem, and; assessing overall project risks.

Most projects within organizations are the result of someone (inside or outside the organization) expressing a desire to have something developed that will make their lives easier. This may seem like a simplistic view of the situation but, when all the fancy language and specifications are stripped from a project request, it usually boils down to, "If I had this, I could do my work better, be more successful, have more free time, make my boss happy, etc." People are frequently looking for personal benefit from the project. You must find out what benefits they expect and develop a project that will provide them.

Some organizations seem to have an aversion to going through this process. They would rather see something get started rather than spend time trying to detail "why" it should be done. If yours is such an organization, getting the answers to some of these questions may be difficult. However, just because it isn't easy doesn't mean you should skip it. Get as much of the information as you can and think through the rest — from the customer's point of view. The structured process described here should help you through this activity.

This project pre-work process involves seven steps which are detailed below:

- Define the problem.

- Determine Needs and Wants.

- Determine the desired outcome.

- Develop options.

- Compare options to Needs and Wants.

- Assess overall risks.

- Select an option.

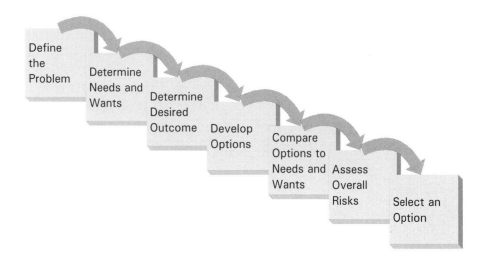

Define the Problem

Understanding "The Problem" is the first step. You must understand, as thoroughly as possible, the problem to be addressed by the project. Some helpful questions to ask at this stage include:

- What are the observable conditions that call attention to this problem? What can be seen and measured to demonstrate that the problem exists?

- What brought this problem to your attention? What happened to make this a priority?

- What is the history of this problem? How long has it been a problem? Has it gotten worse or better recently?

- What are the consequences of not fixing the problem? What is its impact in terms of cost, time, productivity, frustration, etc.?

- Why hasn't this been addressed before? Why is it a priority now?

Try to define the problem in terms that describe the observable situation rather than terms that imply either cause or effect. Be as factual as possible. This may require doing some additional data collection or research in order to develop a clear picture of the situation. The project's customer is likely your best source for this information. It is, after all, probably their problem you are being asked to solve. The project's sponsor is also a good point of reference in this process.

A structured problem-solving process is presented in Appendix A. The process presented is not intended to be used on every problem that arises. It is, however, very good for serious problems that have no readily apparent solutions.

Determine Needs and Wants

When talking with the project's customer and sponsor about the history and background of the problem to be addressed, you can also explore their ideas about what you should do to solve it.

There is a major caution that goes along with this:

> Customers can frequently tell you what they want but they may not be able to tell you what they need. Your job is to find out what they need.

As a starting point, you should ask most of the following questions:

- How do you see the problem? What are your ideas about possible solutions that would fix it?

- Why do you think that would fix it?

- Can you see other alternatives that might also fix the problem?

- How will you measure the success of the solution?

- What are the major requirements for a successful solution?

Armed with this basic information, you can begin to develop a list of Needs and Wants. There is a distinct difference between a "Need" and a "Want." For our purposes here, the following definitions will be used:

- Need – a requirement that must be met by any solution implemented in order for the solution to be viewed as minimally successful.

- Want – a desired outcome of the solution that, while it may be important, is not critical to success.

Using these definitions, it should be clear that Needs are very black and white; they are mandatory for success. If these results are not achieved, if these resources are exceeded, if these policies are violated, etc., the solution is a failure. Needs are either addressed by the solution, in which case the solution meets the minimum requirements for success or, they are not and therefore the solution fails to meet the minimum standards of success.

In defining the Needs, remember to state them in measurable terms. You will need some means of determining whether you have met the Need or not. Try for the most quantifiable measures you can develop. When you are faced with a Need that doesn't lend itself to easily quantifiable measurement, such as "satisfaction" or "ease-of-use," develop a solid set of criteria for determining whether the Need has been met.

Not every project will have Needs as defined here. There are projects that are not driven by absolute necessity. But, most projects have objectives that, while not essential, are nevertheless desirable. These are Wants, and they usually vary in their degree of importance to the project. Therefore, we need an additional classification system for Wants. For example, I want an Italian sports car. I need reliable transportation. The difference between the two is up to $130,000.00 and a live-in mechanic.

A simple and effective means of doing this is weighting: Indicating relative importance on a scale of 10 to 1. The Want that stands out as most important is designated a 10. All other Wants are assessed and weighted relative to that benchmark. In some cases, two or more Wants will be determined to be of equal importance. They are assigned the same weight. A Want assigned a weight of 5 has half the influence of a 10-weighted Want.

Assigning weights to Wants is a subjective process. Several people evaluating the same set of Wants may well give them very different weights depending on the judgment, experience and understanding they bring to the process. It is not a bad idea to pass your list of weighted Wants by one or more people for their input and comment.

Once you've developed and classified your Wants, it's helpful to step back and review them. Make sure the Wants all pertain to the problem statement, and that both short- and long-term issues have been considered. The Wants should be stated clearly so that Needs are measurable and Wants are well defined and weighted.

In order to be useful in evaluating options, a Want should:

• Be stated as an outcome or result and not as a feature.

• Cover one, and only one, aspect of the developing solution. Avoid letting your Wants get "fuzzy" or complex. Keep them simple and clear. Do not mix short-term and long-term Wants.

Determine the Desired Outcome

The first two steps of this process should yield sufficient information to allow you to develop a preliminary statement of the desired outcome of the project, at least in general terms. This is one of the steps in developing the Project Goal statement that will be discussed later in this chapter.

The desired outcome should begin to emerge as you develop and refine your list of Needs and Wants. Those things that are defined as Needs must be part of the final product that is delivered at the end of the project. Those things defined as Wants are of varying importance, but still need to be considered. Try to develop an outcome statement that incorporates the Needs and important Wants. Some examples of outcome statements include:

• Develop and implement a customer feedback process. The process must provide weekly reports on customer responses to questions about service, product quality, and price. The process must have both written (comment card) and telephone interview components. The process must be "user-friendly" (to be defined) for both customers and employees. If possible, the process should allow for both statistical responses and "open-ended comments." It should require no more than three minutes to complete, less than 90 seconds would be best. The process must include a document trail for follow-up and an "alert" system to identify issues that need immediate attention.

- Develop and put in manufacturing a less expensive (to be defined) version of the professional carpenter's hand-saw. The product will be aimed at the mid-level home user. The product should cost at least 20% less to manufacture than the professional model. The blade should test at a minimum of 70% of the current model's hardness and edge-sustaining ability. It can have a plastic handle if this is a significant cost savings. At the very least, a prototype of the product must be available for presentation and demonstration at the National Hardware Show in August.

- Upgrade the accounting application software to include the ability to process and print accounts payable checks. Checks must be run through the current printers. This necessitates locating a vendor who can provide checks that will work. The check program must include all accounting tracking functions such as on-going account balances, sundown dates for uncashed checks, processing deposits and transfers, etc. The system must be secure. The system should have a graphical user interface and display data in a WYSIWYG (what-you-see-is-what-you-get) screen format if possible. All fields must be searchable. The database for the program must interface with the existing accounting database.

None of these are sufficient, as they currently stand, to serve as goal statements for projects. They are mainly lists of necessary and desirable outcomes and characteristics of the final output of the project. They do, however, provide the basis for the remainder of this pre-work analysis.

Develop Options

The next part of the process involves developing options and evaluating alternative means of achieving the Needs and Wants of the project.

The first step in this stage is to list the options from which to make our choice. In some situations you may be presented with a list of acceptable alternatives. Other times, you may have a specific responsibility for generating alternatives.

In some projects the sources for alternatives are clear. For example, a project to plan and put on a company picnic comes with several "assumed" alternatives: It must be accessible to all employees and their families, it should allow for amusements for all ages, it will probably include food and beverages, it should be scheduled on a day when most people can attend, it should have a contingency plan in case of inclement weather, etc. The particulars of most of these will need to be developed but, these basic options are there.

In other situations, we must widen the search for alternatives. In projects where value is placed on a new or different approach, our ability to develop creative alternatives will enhance the quality of the output.

The problem statement clarifies the purpose of the choice and defines the acceptable range of alternatives. If we feel too constrained by the problem as stated, we may need to test our perception of the fundamental purpose and increase or decrease the scope of the project. Increasing the scope broadens the range of alternatives. Decreasing the scope narrows the range.

The list of Needs and Wants also provides a source of alternatives. Each Need or Want in turn can be used to generate possible choices. Focusing on the satisfaction of only one Need or Want at a time can free our creativity.

When only a narrow range of options appears to exist, these can be modified, improved, adapted and combined. For example, the unique features of two alternatives can be combined to create a third. This will provide additional options within the boundaries set by the problem statement.

Generating options is a creative step. We should therefore use any method or technique that releases our creativity.

Compare Options to Needs and Wants

Once options are listed, you can begin the process of seeing how they perform against the Needs and Wants. Base your assessment on the best available information about each option. In addition to known facts, this information may take the form of your best projections or the opinion of experts. The Needs and Wants serve as the guide for your data gathering. For each Need and Want, you must have complete information about all of the options, so that you can make a reasonable judgment.

Begin with the Needs. If your statement of desired outcome has identified Needs, you can use these to screen out those options that fail to meet these minimum requirements. When an option does not meet a Need, drop it as a possible choice. There is nothing to be gained from considering it further. (If there are no Needs, all options will be evaluated against the Wants.)

If all options are eliminated when compared to the Needs, you can take several actions. You can choose to develop additional options, or review both the problem statement and Needs to see if a realistic choice is even possible. It may be necessary to change the requirements of the Needs or to broaden the scope of the project.

You can now analyze which of the remaining alternatives best satisfy the Wants. Again, to do this effectively, you must depend on gathering quality information about each alternative.

You may wish to make visible your judgment on each alternative by using a scoring system. You can use the same 10 to 1 scale used in weighting the Wants. For each Want in turn, compare the information on the options to determine which one best satisfies that Want. This alternative receives a score of 10. The other alternatives are scored relative to the alternative that scored the 10. It is sometimes helpful to do the scoring without having the weights of the Wants visible. One tool for making this comparison is an Alternative Rating Form.

The sample below shows how to use an Alternative Rating Form to evaluate options against Wants. This form is useful for comparing a series of options against all the Wants at once.

Once the scoring is complete, you can calculate the weighted score, which is simply a multiplication of the weight by the score. The numbers help make visible your judgment of two dimensions: How important each Want is for the overall project and which option best satisfies each Want. When the weighted scores are totaled for each alternative, you have a clear comparison of the performance of the alternatives.

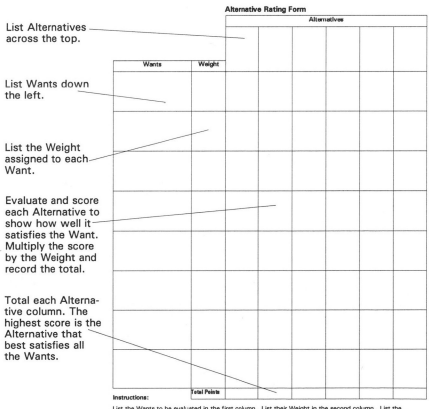

List Alternatives across the top.

List Wants down the left.

List the Weight assigned to each Want.

Evaluate and score each Alternative to show how well it satisfies the Want. Multiply the score by the Weight and record the total.

Total each Alternative column. The highest score is the Alternative that best satisfies all the Wants.

Alternative Rating Form

Alternatives

Wants | Weight

Total Points

Instructions:

List the Wants to be evaluated in the first column. List their Weight in the second column. List the Alternatives to be compared across the top. Work across, evaluating each Alternative against each Want, one at a time. Assign a score to each Alternative that reflects how well it satisfies the Want. Multiply the score by the Weight for that Want. Enter the total in the Alternative column. Total each Alternative column.

Because the comparison of options depends on your ability to accurately assess the information, you need to make every effort to ensure that the information is complete and correct. Even with the same data available, interpretations may differ slightly based on people's different backgrounds, experience, values and responsibility in the project. Significant differences in viewpoint should be explored, since they most likely arise from unclear or inadequate information or a disagreement about the meaning of a Want.

The total weighted score makes visible your judgment about which alternatives best satisfy your Wants. Those that failed to pass the Need screening have been eliminated. The alternatives you eliminate now will be those with the poorest total weighted scores. Those alternatives closely clustered with the highest scoring alternative should now be reviewed for inherent risk. While you should consider the risks involved in choosing any of the alternatives left after the Need screen, it will save time and effort to focus only on those that seem most promising.

Assess Overall Project Risks

" "

Jack the python got loose again. Don't go in there alone. It takes two to handle him.

Note on the front door of a hunter's cabin in the Western United States

Considering the risks associated with the remaining options is the next step of this process. By imagining that the option you are considering has been selected, anticipate what might go wrong during its implementation. You can draw on your own experience and that of others. The information accumulated in comparing options against Needs and Wants may also provide a source of future risks. In this step, you are trying to answer the questions: "What problems might we encounter?," and "What effects might these have?."

All projects have risks associated with them. The fact that you are undertaking something new carries inherent risk. It is the type and severity of the risk that you should be concerned with at this point.

Risk is exposure to the possibility of economic or financial loss or gain, physical damage or injury, or delay, as a consequence of the uncertainty associated with pursuing a particular course of action.

Risk analysis can involve a number of approaches to dealing with the problems created by uncertainty, including the identification, evaluation, control, and management of risk.

Significant Project Risks

" "

Take calculated risks. That is quite different from being rash.

George S. Patton
1885-1945
General, U.S. Army

While all projects carry some level of risk, certain characteristics of either the project or the circumstances under which the project is to be completed increase the potential for severe adverse consequences. Risk increases significantly when projects involve:

• Large capital outlays. Expensive projects are risky projects. If the organization is going to expend significant amounts of money, the organization is going to expect significant return on that investment. As long as the need for the expenditure is clearly stated and understood at the outset, this risk is manageable.

- Unbalanced cash-flow. This is another aspect of large capital outlays. Some projects require a large proportion of the total investment to be expended before any returns are obtained. New product development projects are excellent examples of this type of risk. In new product development projects, virtually all the development and start-up manufacturing expenses are incurred with the expectation that, when the product hits the market, these expenses (and a substantial profit) can be recovered. Impatience and "cutting corners to save money" are the greatest threats to these projects.

- Significant new technology. There are two aspects to this issue. The first is the most obvious: If you are among the first to adopt a new technology, you are at risk. You may be the one to discover the "fatal" bug in the technology. Being the Beta-test site for that new software may be fun and exciting but, if you need the software to be fully operational when you use it, waiting until it has been reviewed, revised, and reissued may be a better course of action.

  The second aspect of new technology risk involves being the first in your organization to adopt a new technology. Even if the technology is not all that "new" to others, it may be very new to you and your organization. The learning curve on new technologies can be very steep. This must be factored into any plans to adopt a new technology.

- Stringent legal, insurance, contractual, regulatory or licensing requirements. These usually involve constraints placed on the project from outside the organization.

  - In the case of legal issues, projects that butt up against copyright and patent issues are risky.

  - Insurance issues come in two basic varieties: Protection and performance bonds. In the case of protection, a project that requires special insurance to guard against loss or damage is more risk-prone than one that does not. In the case of performance bonds, if the project is not completed in conformance to the bond, the bond is forfeited.

  - Contractual issues can be as simple as "no delivery, no money," or they can involve penalties (sometimes into the thousands of dollars an hour range) for late delivery. It is also possible to have rewards for early delivery written into contracts but this is more rare.

  - Regulatory requirements are a common issue in government projects. Documentation and reporting requirements are frequently included in contracts issued by the government. Regulations can also involve most of the other issues in this list such as performance bonds and special insurance requirements and legal issues such as EEO (Equal Employment Opportunity and Minority Business participation) and ADA (Americans with Disabilities Act) compliance.

- Licensing issues are somewhat less common unless the project involves the use of someone else's proprietary property such as the use of a patented product or process or copyrighted material.

- Sensitive environmental or safety issues. Both of these are common in construction projects. They may also be of concern in product or process development projects, particularly when the project involves the use of dangerous or hazardous materials or processes.

In most cases, the risks faced by project leaders inside organizations are not of a catastrophic nature. This does not mean that risks do not exist, only that they are not generally of a magnitude sufficient to justify a full-scale risk-engineering approach to their identification and analysis.

What most project managers face are the risks associated with the inability to accurately and consistently forecast the future. It is difficult to anticipate every situation that may arise in the course of a project and, it is not really necessary. What you must do, however, is to examine your projects for those situations which present greater than average uncertainty and to plan what you will do if the worst (or the very bad) happens.

There is another level of risk that is very important to the success of a project. This is the issue of the risks that are encountered as the project is being implemented. This issue is discussed in detail in Chapter 4: **Project Planning**, under the heading Contingency Planning.

To complete this discussion of overall project risk, we need to have some way of determining the potential impact of an identified risk.

For each identified risk you need to evaluate two conditions:

- The probability that the identified risk will materialize — that something will go wrong, and

- The impact on the project if it does go wrong.

The first of these, determining probability, is really a judgment call on the part of the project team. Try to use as much information as you can about past projects with similar conditions but also rely on your "gut feeling" for how likely a potential problem is. Rate the probability as either "Low," "Medium," or "High."

The second evaluation can be based on much more concrete information. What will it mean to the project if the problem occurs? How bad will it be? Can you recover from it or will you have to start over? Also rate this as either "Low," "Medium," or "High."

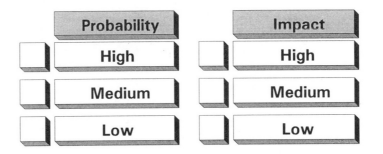

Now comes another judgment call. If both the probability and the impact are rated as "High," you have a built-in problem.

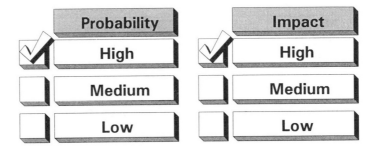

This situation alone may be enough to eliminate an alternative from consideration.

If the probability is rated "Medium" and the impact is rated "High,"

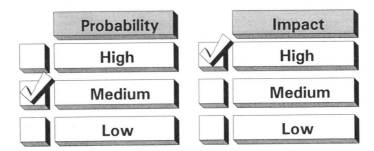

this alternative should be very carefully evaluated. Anything that can be done to minimize either the probability or the impact, or both, should be considered before the project is started.

If, on the other hand, the probability is rated "Low" and the impact is rated "High,"

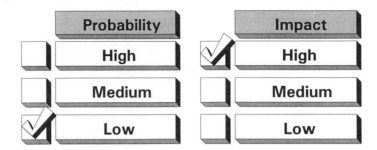

you have a judgment call to make. Should you worry about a low-probability risk even though it might have severe consequences? Is it really a low probability? What can you do to further lower the likelihood of it happening?

On the other side of the scale, a "High" probability connected with a "Low" impact,

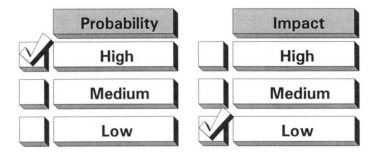

may indicate an issue that can be avoided by careful planning. If you know the problem is likely to occur, even though it is not expected to cause severe problems, why not simply plan around it?

The instances of "Medium" probability and "Medium" impact are also in the judgment-call arena. If it worries you, try planning around it. If it doesn't, don't.

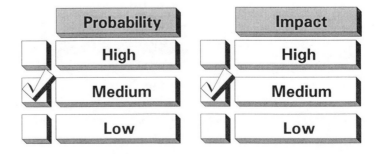

Select an Option

Having defined the problem, established Needs and Wants, clarified the desired outcome of the project, developed options and screened them through the Needs and Wants, and finally assessed the risks associated with each option, you are in a position to select the option that will become the project.

By this point, the choice should be fairly obvious. If the option that scored best in meeting the Wants as identified also has the lowest associated risk, it is probably your best choice. If, however, the option that scored best in meeting the Wants has an unacceptable level of risk, another option, one that possibly meets fewer of the Wants, may be a better choice. At least, having done this pre-work, you have the information to make a good decision.

Developing the Project Goal

" "

Any company needs a strong, unifying sense of direction. But that need is particularly strong in an organization in which tasks are differentiated and responsibilities dispersed.

Chris A. Bartlett
Harvard Business School

Using the information gathered in the needs analysis process, you are now ready to work on the goal statement for the project.

Project goals need not be complex, excessively detailed or long. They should, however, clearly state the desired outcome of the project in a way that can be used to guide and drive the project.

Virtually everything about building a goal statement centers around negotiations with management and various stakeholders in the project. You are trying to gain agreements and commitments from everyone affected by the project that what you propose to do, how you propose to go about it, the criteria for success, the resource requirements and the time-frame for completion are all acceptable.

The primary tool for these negotiations is the project goal statement. Setting a clear project goal is a critical activity at the beginning of a project.

In setting a project goal you are trying to do two things:

* Focus yourself and your team on the target.

* Create commitment to, and agreement about, that target.

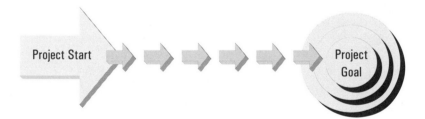

Frequently, project leaders complain that they cannot get good direction from management: "They can tell me what they *don't* want but not what they *do* want." This is one of the reasons for going through the needs analysis process described earlier. Clear goals are the result of a process. It is a process that takes time, energy and dialogue. It is a process of going back and forth with other people, working toward clarity of direction for the project — in short, it is a process of negotiation.

Since projects tend to be unique, it is often difficult to be clear on a goal from the very beginning. Since goal setting is a process of dialogue, it can start in one of two ways:

* Management can tell you what they see as the project goal.

* You can tell management what you see as the project goal.

It is always easier to edit than it is to create. So, develop a draft goal statement. Take it to one or more of the project's stakeholders and say, "Here, this is what I think the project goal is." This gives them the option to say, "Yes, that's the goal. Proceed." or "No, that's not what I meant. Here's what I meant." You go back and forth as you move closer to achieving clarity about the direction and the expected end result of the project.

One way to look at a project goal is as a statement of project output: How will we know we are finished? What will the end result look like? Try to put the goal in user terms. Who is the user of your project's output? What does your user — client, customer, manager — want from you? What does the end user say you are supposed to be doing?

A user doesn't care that you are trying to produce a new accounting system. The user cares about obtaining certain information about inventory and sales at the end of the day. Providing a system that meets the user's needs is your goal; designing a new accounting system is your process for doing this. Putting yourself on the user's side improves your chances of hitting the target.

Effective project leaders always try to include the end user in the project, or at least to imagine the user's point of view.

SMART Goals

" "

Fixing your objective is like identifying the North Star — you sight your compass on it and then use it as the means of getting back on the track when you stray.

Marshall E. Dimock
Author

One of the largest projects in human history was undertaken based on one simple statement:

"I believe this country should dedicate itself to the task, before this decade is out, of sending a man to the moon and returning him safely to earth."

President John F. Kennedy, 1962

The scope of activity this simple statement created is almost unprecedented in human history. Whole industries came into being as a result of this goal statement.

While most of your projects won't result in the level of national activity that Kennedy's statement caused, you should give it a great deal of thought. A good goal statement makes the rest of the project planning process, and the actual work on the project much easier to manage.

Good goals are SMART goals. In addition to being established in terms of the user, an effective project goal has five characteristics. The acronym SMART captures the characteristics of a goal that is likely to provide focus and create commitment. SMART goals are:

- Specific.

- Measurable.

- Agreed upon.

- Realistic.

- Time-framed.

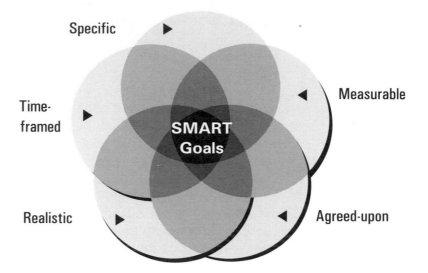

Specific

Your goal should be so specific, so well defined, so clear that any-body with some basic knowledge of the project area can read it, un-derstand it, and know what you are trying to accomplish. You could leave the company tomorrow and somebody else could pick up the statement of your project's goal and know exactly what to do.

This is the statement of Output from the triple constraint. As clearly as possible, it should state exactly what will be delivered at the end of the project.

Measurable

If you can't measure it, you can't manage it. To manage a project to successful completion, you have to be able to measure the goal. It's been said — wrongly — that some project goals cannot be measured. Of course, some goals can be measured more easily than others but, all goals need to be measurable. In fact, developing clear measuring standards for the most ambiguous and fuzzy kinds of goals is where you should spend the most time. Without measurable goals, project team members cannot get any sense of direction, and they wind up shooting at the wrong target. Project participants need to work on measurable activities, even if the measures are crude, in order to know what to do. And you need a measurable goal if you are to man-age it.

Give people a target they can aim at. They should also be able to measure their own progress. Having clear measurement criteria is a vital part of the process of setting good goals.

Avoid vague terms like "quicker," "cheaper," "more productive." Use quantifiable measures like, "reduce process time by 18%"; "reduce cost by 21%"; "improve productivity by reducing rework by 80%, increasing output by 20% and reducing scrap by 90%."

Even the fuzziest goals should have measures. Customer satisfaction and employee-morale goals may seem hard to measure but there are ways. For example, customer satisfaction can be measured by tracking complaints and compliments, returns, warranty claims, service calls, etc. Employee morale can be measured by surveys and interviews. Find the measures that will allow you to determine your success at meeting the goal and include them in it.

Agreed Upon

" "

Assumption is the mother of screw-up.
Angelo Donghia
1935-1985
American Designer

There must be agreement about the project's goals. The end user, be it a customer, upper management, or a subordinate in the organization, must agree that the achievement of the project's goal is necessary and desirable. Stated differently, the project leader and the project's stakeholders must agree that the end result should solve the problem or respond to the need that led to the initiation of the project. The more people agree and have clarified the goal up front, the easier it will be to develop a viable plan for the project. This agreement will make it easier to respond to changes that may require modifying the goal as the project unfolds. Agreement is based on sharing information, and it builds commitment toward the project.

As stated in Section 1, the connection of the project's goal to some other goal in the organization is a critical element for gaining the necessary support. The clearer the connection between the project goal and the organizational goal, the better. This also makes negotiation about the project much easier since you already have common ground on which to build.

Realistic

" "

You cannot seek for the ideal outside the realm of reality.
Leon Blum
1872-1949
Premier of France

Project goals must be realistic. Realistic is not a synonym for "easy." Most projects will challenge the participants. The project may well require that they do things they've never done before; think more creatively than usual; experiment with new approaches, techniques and ideas. This does not mean accomplishing the goal is impossible — just more difficult than doing your everyday work. Even though the project is unique and different from what may have been done before, it should not be totally alien to project personnel. If it is, you are asking for trouble. If this is the case, you will need to set aside time for research and learning, or perhaps engage consultants or hire new project team members or even delay the project. You should not get trapped into doing things you know little about, unless you love the smell of your own adrenaline or don't mind failing. This is the wisdom of "stick to your knitting," which successful companies follow. Do the things with which you have some experience. The goal-setting process should help you clarify this issue.

Realism also includes the resources available for completing the project. All too often project leaders agree to goals that are impossible to achieve, given the resources, knowledge and time available. Such project leaders set themselves up for frustration and failure. How many times have you been assigned a project and a deadline before the goal is clarified, only to find out that the project cannot possibly be completed on time? One of the benefits you derive from dialogue in the goal-setting process is determining whether you are talking about a goal that is realistic, given your time and resources. You have to question this assumption explicitly. Don't just say, "Sure, we can get that done." Discuss resources, personnel and timing to determine how realistic the goal is. Making it realistic may mean adjusting the goal, the deadline or the resources.

Time-Framed

" "

The ultimate inspiration is the deadline.

Nolan Bushnell
Founder, Atari

Finally, you need a clear time frame for the goal. How much time and budget do you have to accomplish this project? Is there any flexibility in the deadline? Is there any flexibility in the resources available for the project? This goes back to looking at what is attainable. You want to set a deadline that is reasonable, given the resources available and the amount of knowledge and experience you have with this type of project.

Testing the Goal Against the Criteria

Let's look at the Kennedy goal statement in the light of the SMART criteria.

- Specific:
    - Send a man to the moon.
    - Return him to Earth.
    - Alive.

- Measurable:
    - Man arrives on the moon.
    - Man returns to earth.
    - Man is still alive upon landing.

- Agreed-upon:

    - There are several factors that impacted this criteria with regard to the Apollo project. First of all, there was never universal agreement that the moon landing was a necessary or desirable goal. There was however, sufficient agreement among the primary stakeholders — the military, the Washington establishment, and the scientific community — to carry the day. Among the population at large, enthusiasm and agreement varied widely. The portions of the population that agreed were very vocal in their support. The portions that disagreed, while they outnumbered the supporters by a significant margin, were disorganized and unfocused.

- Another set of factors that had a significant impact on the acceptance of this goal was the world political situation. In 1957, the Soviet Union launched Sputnik I, the first artificial satellite. The U.S. followed six months later, in February, 1958, by launching its first satellite. The Russians countered by sending a dog into space and, in September, 1959, landed (well, crashed, actually) the first spacecraft, Luna 2, on the moon. The U.S. followed by sending up a monkey. Then, in April, 1961 the Soviets sent the first man, Yuri Gagarin, into space. The U.S. followed in February, 1962, by sending John Glenn up to be the first man to orbit the globe. There is one central theme through all of this. It is embodied in the phrase "...the U.S. followed...." This was a situation we, as a nation, were not happy about. We did not deal well with being Number Two. Particularly not behind the Soviet Union. This situation, coupled with the general paranoia about what the Russians would do if they got to the moon first, provided most of the impetus needed to push the Apollo project forward.

- Realistic:

  - Much of the technology needed for the moon shot existed in 1962. We had the rocket and basic guidance technology to get a ship to the moon. By 1962, we had sent up and retrieved several satellites and had proven that a man could survive re-entry. Some of the problems that still needed solving included the part about a soft landing on the moon's surface and that sticky problem of lifting off and returning to earth. Kennedy's science advisors were convinced that, with enough money and manpower, these problems could be solved and, so the Apollo project was launched.

- Time-framed:

  - By the end of this decade. Not only did we meet this deadline, we actually exceeded it by several months — July 21, 1969.

A Goal-Statement-Development Process

" "

Writing is easy. All you have to do is sit staring at a blank sheet of paper until the drops of blood form on your forehead.

Gene Fowler
American Writer

If you've ever tried to just sit down and write a goal statement you know that it is not all that easy. Some people agonize over them for days. At this stage of the project, you don't need a goal statement that will win the inspirational literature prize. You need a working statement that can serve as a solid starting point for your project.

If you are fortunate enough to have access to some of the people who will ultimately work on your project, try the following process and see if it doesn't help speed up the process of developing a draft goal statement.

Bring the group together in a room with a flip chart and a couple of pads of self-stick notes (such as Post-it® Notes from 3-M Corporation). Get the group talking about the project and what needs to be done. Don't try to guide the discussion too much. As people talk about what the project entails, capture key words and phrases on individual self-stick notes. When you've gotten several pieces, stick them randomly on the flip chart. Let the group go until they begin to run down.

When the flow of ideas starts to slow down, try arranging the words and phrases you've captured into basic pieces of sentences. You'll be missing most of the connecting words like "the," "and," "with," etc. and you can add these if you wish. Step back from your draft and ask whether it looks like a goal statement that could be used to get the project started. The answer will likely be that it doesn't really look like that yet but, most of the pieces are likely to be there as a starting point. From there on, it is simply a matter of refining and fine-tuning what you have as a beginning.

This process is a variation on brainstorming and, like brainstorming, a little practice and experience makes it easier to use. A few tips can make this process work smoother:

- Keep in mind that your project will have a beginning, a middle and an end. Try to arrange the pieces of your goal statement in that order. Start with the biggest pieces of the project and work toward the details.

- It is sometimes helpful to provide the opening few words for the developing statement such as: "Design and build...," or "Research, design and implement...," or "Specify, purchase and install...." This can get the group focused on the overall purpose of the project rather than all the details of doing it.

- Try several arrangements of the pieces. One of the advantages of using self-stick notes is that they are almost infinitely movable. Try grouping similar parts together and working on them as individual sentences within the overall goal statement. Try rearranging the order of words within your developing sentences.

- When reviewing the developing goal statement, read it out loud. You can add the missing conjunctions as you read it. This also helps people get a "feel" for the spirit, power, and effectiveness of the words being used.

- Don't throw away any of the notes until you're certain you won't need them. Simply remove them from the working page of the flip chart but keep them handy. You will find that you may need them as the statement begins to get refined.

- Ask frequently if the statement is developing into something that could be used to drive the project. This helps keep the group focused on the purpose of the exercise and keeps the process moving. This whole activity should only take between ten and twenty minutes.

• When you and the group are satisfied with what you have developed, write it down and use it as your draft goal statement.

It can help to give the group a starting point such as "Develop, test and implement...", or "Research, design, build and install..." Write the individual words on separate Post-it® Notes and put them on a flipchart or other surface the whole group can see. Have the group brainstorm about the project. Capture key words and phrases as the group says them. Write them on individual Post-it® Notes and post them randomly on the page.

Once you have a fair number of pieces, try arranging them into logical groups such as phases of the project, groups of tasks, key ideas, etc. There will likely be missing pieces but don't worry about them at this time. Try reading what you've created. You may have to fill in some of the blanks to have it make any sense.

Add detail on additional Post-it® Notes to flesh out the statement.

Try various arrangements of the emerging sentences. Read each version out loud for the group. Continue to add detail and missing pieces.

You can add the connector words such as "and", "the", "or", "a", etc. if desired.

After about four or five passes, you should have a workable draft of a goal statement.

Uses for the Project Goal Statement

" "

Capture inter-office supporters by involving them in developmental goals and programs. It gives others a vested interest in speeding up the approval process.

Terry Ware
U. S. Government Printing Office

The project goal statement is a powerful tool throughout the life of the project. It is the benchmark against which every activity, every decision, every deliverable is measured.

In the process of negotiating for goal approval you need to remember that it isn't just the approval of management that is needed. You need the commitment of everyone who will be affected by the project. This can be a tedious process, especially on very large projects or on projects that have far-reaching impacts.

Unfortunately, there is no simple way to achieve this commitment. It requires one-on-one meetings between the project leader and the individuals from whom the commitment is needed.

There are two things to keep in mind when approaching people for commitment:

- What's in it for them?

  - If you are asking someone for support for the project (either through supplying resources or personnel, or by providing expertise), you should try to find some benefit for them which will help compensate them for their support.

- What, exactly, are you asking them to do?

  - Be as specific as possible. You are asking them to agree to some form of support. Be sure they understand exactly what that support is to be, when you expect it, how long you will need it, what you plan to do with it, etc.

The project goal statement is an excellent tool to use when negotiating support. If it is well defined, the benefits to the organization (and the individuals within the organization) should be fairly clear.

There is more on the subject of Negotiation in Chapter 3: **People Skills for Project Leaders**.

Detailing commitment

A Commitment Form is a simple tool for outlining who supports, who opposes, and who is neutral about your project. It can also spur the planning about how you will gain the commitment and cooperation of the various people connected with the project.

The form that follows is a simple list of who you need commitment from, what commitment you need from them, and where you believe they stand at the moment (for, against, or unsure).

This is not a "hard" scientific tool based on verifiable data. It is based on your perceptions of where specific people stand in relation to the project. It is also not necessarily a tool for publication. You may want to use it to simply identify who needs to support your project, in what way and where you think they stand at the moment.

This is a tool for developing strategy. How will you strengthen the commitment of those who already support your project? How will you convert the "unsure" into supporters (or at least keep them from going over to the "against" side)? What can you do to change the minds of those who are against it? Or, if you can't change their position, how can you minimize their ability to negatively impact the project?

Commitment Analysis Form

Project: _____ Date: _____
                                    Project Manager: _____
                                    Project Sponsor: _____

List individuals from whom commitment or support is needed down the left.

Indicate the specific commitment or support needed from them.

Check whether you believe they are: "For," "Against," or "Unsure" regarding your project.

Use this information to develop strategies for:
1) Strengthening existing commitment,
2) insuring those who are "Unsure", at worst, remain neutral, and at best become "For," and,
3) overcoming objections.

Individual	Commitment Needed	For	Against	Unsure

Determining the Skills Needed for the Project

" "

You can dream, create, design, and build the most wonderful place in the world, but it requires people to make the dream a reality.

Walt Disney
1901-1966
American Film Producer

With the project goal and much of the pre-work completed, you should have an idea of the skills that will be needed to complete the project. In some organizations, project team members are assigned right along with the project leader. When people are assigned to a project team they are frequently chosen based on general knowledge of the project work and, most importantly, their availability. This does not always yield the people most qualified to do the work.

The Skills and Influence Matrix can be used to identify the skills needed to accomplish the work and show which team members have which skill sets. It can show when skills are duplicated in several team members. It can also show when critical skills are missing completely. This is a tool that can be used in negotiations for people with those necessary skills.

Like most of the tools in this book, this one works best when it is used by the team rather than by an individual. Ask for input from team members about their strengths and weaknesses. You may find some surprising talents you didn't know were there.

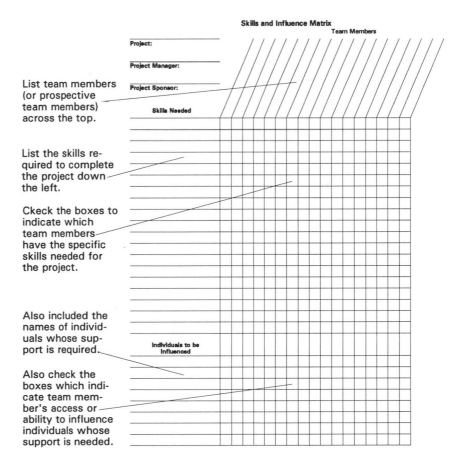

List team members (or prospective team members) across the top.

List the skills required to complete the project down the left.

Ckeck the boxes to indicate which team members have the specific skills needed for the project.

Also included the names of individuals whose support is required.

Also check the boxes which indicate team member's access or ability to influence individuals whose support is needed.

Assembling the Project Team

Once the people with the skills and influences needed for the project have been identified, you can begin to assemble the project team. Project teams usually consist of three distinct types of members:

- Core team members — those with essential skills and with whom you will likely share some task management responsibilities.

- Project team members — the individuals whose expertise is needed throughout the life of the project in order to accomplish the project's objectives and goal.

- Project supporters — individuals whose expertise is only required at certain points in the project and who do not participate in most other activities.

Most projects within organizations are not staffed by "dedicated" personnel — people assigned full-time to the project. They tend to be staffed by "borrowed" personnel — people who still have other jobs and who work on the project in addition to other duties.

This creates a tendency toward "dual loyalty" on the part of team members. People will tend to give more weight to the desires of those who can directly affect their careers, i.e., their managers.

This presents some interesting challenges for project leaders. Most projects operate outside the functional lines of authority and power of the organization. This means that most project leaders do not have direct authority over the individuals on the project team. They don't write their performance reviews, grant raises, etc. This puts the project leader in an interesting position when it comes to ensuring continued support and cooperation.

Project leaders who find themselves in this situation need to exercise some sophisticated negotiation skills when building their project teams. (See "Negotiation" in Section 3: **People Skills for Project Leaders**.) You should negotiate for several specific commitments from both the potential team member and that person's functional manager.

- A commitment to the goal of the project. If they are going to work on the project, they should be committed to its success. They should "buy in" to the goal and understand its implications and importance.

- A commitment to the tasks and activities for which they will be responsible. By assembling most of the team prior to beginning the detailed planning of the project, you have an excellent opportunity to build commitment through the planning process itself.

People are more likely to commit and follow through on tasks they have helped design than they are on those that are simply assigned to them.

- A realistic assessment of the time that the team member can devote to the project. The key word here is "realistic." How much time can the person actually devote to the project, given all the other duties and responsibilities they have? There is a tendency for people to over-estimate when they are excited about a project and to under-estimate when they are not. You may need to do some verification of their estimates.

- An understanding of functional responsibilities that may cause scheduling conflicts with the project. You need to know those activities and tasks that are likely to require significant or recurring allocations of the person's time. These can be things like mandatory weekly staff meetings; daily or weekly tasks that must be done regularly; commitments to other projects; etc.

From the functional manager, you need

&6 99

A person usually has two reasons for doing something; a good reason and the real reason.

J. Pierpont Morgan
American Financier

- A commitment to support the activities of his or her employees working on the project. This is important. There will almost certainly be times when the needs of the functional area and the needs of the project will conflict. The last thing you want to happen is to put the employee in the middle of this kind of conflict. A commitment of support up front goes a long way toward ensuring that this doesn't happen.

- An agreement that the project is important and that the employee's participation is required in order to accomplish the project goal. What you're asking for here is agreement about the project's goal. The more closely connected the project goal is to some goal of the manager's, the better.

- A realistic assessment of the time the employee can devote to the project and still perform his or her functional duties. This can provide the verification of what the employee estimated about their availability. If there is a big discrepancy between the two estimates (the employee's and the manager's), discuss it with the employee.

- An agreement about how conflicts between the needs of the project and the needs of the functional department will be settled. This is an acknowledgment of the fact that you know there will be times when the needs of the project and the needs of the functional group will conflict. The most common response from managers to this is, "We'll talk it out and reach a decision." This usually means the manager wins. This is actually how it should be in most cases. The needs of the functional operations of the business almost always supersede the needs of projects within those businesses. All you want to do here is acknowledge the probability of conflict and set the stage for bringing the discussion into the open.

- An agreement that you can provide some degree of input into the performance evaluation of the employee with regard to their work on the project. This is almost always met with something like, "No, that's my job." Don't argue with this. In many instances, the manager is right. The exceptions to this are projects that truly stretch an employee's skills and abilities, or projects that involve significant portions of an employee's time. When people have an opportunity to work in a new and different environment; when they have a chance to use skills they don't usually get to use; when they have performed exceptionally well; they need to be recognized.

  There is a simple way to input to someone's performance record without violating your agreement with that person's manager. At the end of the project, write a "thank you" letter to the manager in which you express your gratitude for his or her support and list the accomplishments of his or her employees. Copy this letter to the employee's personnel file.

These agreements need to be developed and agreed to by everyone who functionally manages members of the project team.

If you are in the same boat — still performing functional duties in addition to your project management duties — you should negotiate the same agreements with your manager.

Deliverables at this Point

For most projects, there are several deliverables at this first milestone:

- The output of the Needs Analysis (Needs and Wants, the ranking of the Wants, assessment of risks, etc.) with whatever background material is needed to justify your conclusions. It is a good idea to have this work reviewed by others to verify your findings and to clarify any unclear information.

- A good draft of the project goal statement (with whatever background material is needed to justify the constraints represented by the statement).

- A list of potential team members and the justification (through the Skills and Influence Matrix) for why each person has been chosen.

- A request for the preliminary resources needed to effectively begin planning the project.

The first three of these have been described earlier in this chapter. The resource request needs some clarification.

A resource request can be as simple as "I need about four hours I can dedicate to outlining this project," or as detailed as a request for: spending authority to hire outside expertise to help define the technical aspects of the project; assignment of personnel to the planning team; preliminary market studies; research; etc. Most projects conducted within an organization tend to fall closer to the first option.

Most internal projects are just that — internal. They utilize the existing resources of the company in various ways. They don't require extensive (and expensive) outside consultations, elaborate research or, large staffs to get them started (or to get them completed for that matter). They all do, however, require some level of preliminary planning in order to get them started effectively.

Whether your request is for an agreement that a few hours of your own time should be allocated to the preliminary planning process or that two people from R&D, one marketing representative, three technical experts and a consultant should be dedicated to the process, the request must be firmly grounded in a documented Need.

This is your first opportunity (the first of many) to admit what you don't know about the project. It is a virtual certainty that there is some aspect of the project that falls completely outside your experience. This is the point at which you should admit it and ask that the appropriate help be provided.

Issues by Project Type

There are some special concerns that surface depending on the type of project being undertaken. These are issues the project leader should watch carefully during this period.

Process Projects

In process development projects (primarily internally-focused), most of the concerns at this stage involve clearly defining the impact of the proposed project on the total work flow of the organization. Specific issues include:

- Determining the actual process-needs to be addressed. This is accomplished by working closely with the ultimate users.

- Determining the potential impact of a process change on other processes. This involves working with both the ultimate users and representatives of all the areas that may be impacted by a change (those which precede, follow and work in parallel with the process being changed).

- Determining the input and output constraints involves careful "mapping" of the total system of which the process is a part.

- Determining the technical constraints around the process requires a solid understanding of the process and the system of which it is a part. You need to know how they work; what the lot-size requirements are; how they inter-relate; what limitations are placed on the process by the total system; new developments in technology which might help or hinder development; etc.

- Determining capital equipment and expense requirements and constraints involves working with various functional groups such as management, purchasing, production planning, facilities, etc., to develop a good "rough draft" or estimate of what capital investments will be needed.

- Obtaining agreement among all parties regarding the proposed process. It is very important that you involve everyone who will be affected by the process in the project to some degree. You will need their cooperation at some point and involving them early and allowing them to state their concerns can prevent massive headaches when it comes to implementation.

- Determining implementation impacts on existing processes. Involving all the players up front can uncover hidden pitfalls that would otherwise surface only after you have tried to make the process operational. This can help you "map" the impacts of the process so you will know what to anticipate at later stages.

• Obtaining input regarding implementation timing, costs, training needs, documentation of the process, etc. All of this information is grist for the planning mill. It is the kind of information you will need in order to complete many of the detail tasks involved in breaking down work into realistic chunks that people can accomplish in a reasonable time-frame.

Product/Service Projects

Product or service development projects are primarily externally-focused. They are directed at providing a response to a perceived need in the external markets of the company. As such, they require the participation of personnel from various internal functions and from the external customer base. (External customers can be represented by marketing and sales personnel from the company — just be sure their information is based on actual customer input, not just "hunches" about what customers want.) Specific issues include:

• Determining market need based on actual customer input can require conducting market studies, interviewing customers, analyzing competitive offerings, examining market trends, etc.

• Determining market size, competitive offerings, pricing constraints, delivery systems, etc., almost always involves direct contact with both the market and with various parts of the product or service delivery system. Some special expertise is required to gather useful data and, if not available internally, this expertise is usually hired from outside the company.

• Profit potential analysis is the process of forecasting the likelihood that the company will show a profit as a result of undertaking the project. This process yields many of the elements of the Triple Constraint by placing limits around the capital investment (and on-going production costs) that are realistic given the potential for profit and by specifying the size of the "window of opportunity" that must be met to optimize profit.

• Establishing a connection between the proposed product or service and the current offerings of the organization. This is more important than it might seem on the surface. Companies get themselves into serious trouble when they "go too far afield" with new product or service offerings. If your business is hardware, expanding into painting supplies or building materials is a reasonable undertaking. Your existing customers are likely to believe that you have the expertise to market these products; you will potentially attract new customers for all your product lines since they are all inter-related. However, if your business is hardware and you expand into the fast food business, few will believe you know what you are doing; there is no reason to believe you can effectively operate in a market totally outside your proven expertise. There must be some realistic connection between the proposed product or service and the products and services you currently offer.

- Determining the technology constraints around the development process and the manufacturing or service delivery process should begin at this stage. It is unlikely that all the constraints will be anticipated but, a careful examination of probable constraints will set you on the right track for additional investigation as the project progresses.

- Obtaining agreement among all parties regarding the proposed product or service. Don't forget to involve customers (or representatives of customers) in this process. They are, after all, the ones who must purchase the product or service. Also, be sure to include everyone who must "handle" the product or support the service on its way to the customer.

- Determining probable production requirements. Include everyone, from purchasing and production planning to shipping and distribution, in this information-gathering activity. The last thing you want to happen is to get ready to launch the product and find that you forgot to have the packaging ordered or to notify distribution that there would be additional shipments coming.

- Determining the basic specifications of the proposed product or service. In most cases, this is an activity between the project team and marketing but, don't forget to include key production or support personnel in this development.

- Obtaining input regarding market-introduction timing, packaging and distribution or service delivery, etc. Again, most of this involves marketing but, there are a significant number of other operations that should be consulted.

Software Projects

Software development projects can be either internally- or externally-focused, i.e., development of a program for internal use (such as accounting or inventory-control software) or development of a program package for sale to industry or the public.

Software projects should be driven primarily by the needs of the end user and constrained by the limitation of the hardware systems on which they must operate. Specific issues include:

- Determining the actual need based on input from either the ultimate internal user or from potential customers. Internal users are much easier to find and a representative of the user group makes a good addition to the project team. Gaining input from external customers requires the same expertise and research outlined under the heading "Product/Service Projects" development projects.

- Determining how the user will use the software is part of the basic development of the performance or quality portion of the Triple Constraint. In order to develop software that meets a specific need, you must understand what the user needs the software to do — how the software should make it easier for the user to do something.

- Analysis of existing offerings is an excellent starting point for much of this research. What do existing offerings do well? What do they do poorly? What features are missing? How much do they cost? Are they "user-friendly" or do they require an extensive technical background in either computers or in the area the program addresses? All of these questions, and many more, will provide insights into how to meet the needs of a specific user group.

- Determining platform constraints is a critical early step in defining the project. Unfortunately (from the user's point of view) there is no "standard" operating system or common hardware. Decisions must be made early in the project about which hardware platform most potential users use. The software must then be developed with a clear understanding of the operational constraints of that platform.

- Determining the programming language is a natural outgrowth of selecting a hardware platform and operating system. Each platform and language has its own set of limitations which must be taken into account in the development process.

- Determining the technical constraints of a software project is made more difficult by the constant (almost daily) technical advancements being made in the computer industry. This requires that project leaders on software development projects, and their technical counterparts, constantly research developments in the field.

- Obtaining agreement among all parties regarding the proposed software package. You should not only be concerned with the operational specifications of the software, but also with the training needs (internal) and the documentation required to make it useful. Should there be a demonstration program? Does it need a tutorial? How about after-sale support? What will you do about updates, etc.?

- Determining probable programming requirements in terms of number of hours, lines of code, etc. The best sources for this information are the people who will actually write the software. Actively seek the input of the people who will do the work and of the people (or their representatives) who will use the program.

- Determining the limitations of the proposed software. Set the boundaries of the product. Be very clear about what it must do, what it should do if possible and, what it does not need to do. Pay particular attention to defining what it doesn't need to do. The biggest pitfall in most software development projects is adding "bells and whistles" that don't need to be there.

Chapter 3
People Skills for Project Leaders

3

People Skills for Project Leaders

Introduction

Of all the subjects in this book, this one has no place where it fits neatly in the flow of a normal project. The skills discussed in this chapter are necessary throughout the life of a project.

People are the key ingredient in any project. People will make the plans, perform the work, solve the problems, track the progress, deliver the output. People skills are critical for any successful project leader.

Before getting into project planning and implementation processes, a discussion of working with people on the project team and others within the organization is appropriate.

Project leaders in most organizations are working with borrowed resources — people who are already scheduled by their managers to do work unrelated to the project. Commonly, the people on your project team do not report to you. You don't manage them. You don't write their performance reviews. You can't grant them raises, bonuses or promotions. They work for someone else. You only have them on loan.

In situations like this, you can't manage people in the traditional sense of telling them what to do and expecting that they will do it. You need to manage through influence rather than authority.

The following material covers a wide range of "people" topics. Not all of them will apply to every situation but, the chances are quite good that all of them will apply at one time or another during your career as a project leader.

In this section, we will look at several aspects of working with people, individually and on project teams. There are six subjects which will be discussed:

- The development and use of power and authority.

- Motivation.

- Leadership.

- How teams grow and change over time.

- Negotiation.

- Communication.

The Development and Use of Power and Authority

" "

This is not Burger King! We do not do it your way. This is the county jail. You will do it our way!

Sign in Chicago's Cook County Jail Cafeteria

Everyone wants power. Few people have enough of it — particularly project leaders. Most of us believe our situations would be better if only we had more power.

We associate power with authority and with one's location in the hierarchy of an organization — position power. This limited view of power assumes that power is a fixed-sum commodity and that there is only so much to go around. Effective project leaders understand that power is dynamic, and like electricity it is all around us and almost limitless in its potential. The challenge is to tap into this energy and channel the forces. Like money in a bank, power is a source of credit that expands with use and makes other people feel stronger and richer.

The word "power" means "to be able." Making something happen arises at least as much from personal competencies as it does from resources associated with position. Professor Michael Badawy states in **Developing Managerial Skills in Engineers and Scientists** that, "Of the two types of power, positional and personal, the project leader's authority is actually based on power which largely stems more from his personal abilities and less from his position." Effective project management power is based on an understanding of the reciprocal relationship between leaders and their followers.

Personal power is a set of skills and abilities. It refers to the ways we work with and respond to others in face-to-face situations. It doesn't come from an office. It travels with an individual.

Where Power Comes From

Traditionally, power has been conceptualized as coming from one or more of five sources:

Reward Power is based on our perception that another person has the ability to reward or grant resources that we desire.

Coercive Power is based on our perception that another person has the ability to punish or withhold valued resources from us.

Legitimate Power is based on our internalized belief that another person has the legitimate right to request certain types of actions and that we have a social obligation to comply with the requests. This is often called "institutional power" or "formal authority."

Referent Power is based on our desire to identify with another person's requests and our belief that going along with that person's requests will facilitate a favorable interpersonal relationship and foster mutual respect.

Expert Power is based on our perception that the other person has some special knowledge or information relevant to the task or problem at hand.

The first three sources: Reward, coercive and legitimate power, form the basis of position power. They are lodged in the position that the person holds. The last two: Referent and expert power, form the sources of personal power. They reside in the personal characteristics of the position holder. There are limits to the amount of position power that you can hold. There are no limits to personal power.

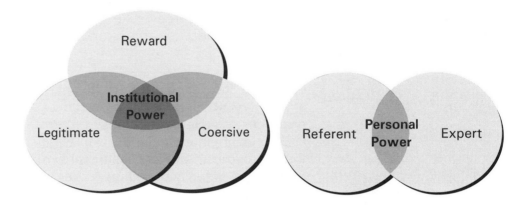

How Power is Distributed

The difference in the effectiveness of two similar operations within a business has been found by researchers to be linked to the distribution of power.

A consistent finding is that managers in the under-achieving areas hoard power. In the high-performing areas, the managers share power. As a result, the people at every level on the high-performing area feel that they can, and should, be responsible for the area's effectiveness. Contemporary management thinking has found the old saying "Power corrupts" to be untrue. In fact, it is now believed that "Powerlessness corrupts" in a more damaging way.

Consider New United Motors Manufacturing, Inc. in Freemont, California, a joint venture between General Motors and Toyota. Any worker in the plant can stop the production line if something doesn't seem right. Any worker can confront a supplier if the supplier's parts are not up to standards. Any worker can go to the president of the plant for direct assistance in maintaining the quality of the Chevrolet Novas manufactured there. When people feel they have power, they feel that they can make a difference and productivity improves.

Another study of project leaders reported several significant relationships between project performance and the use of various power bases. For example, the less project personnel perceived project leaders as using position power and the more they perceived them using personal power, the greater were the levels of project involvement and openness of upward communication and the higher the productivity of the project team. The openness of upward communication is critical to a project leader. Without open, honest communication about what is happening at all levels of the project, a project leader cannot possibly be effective. Similar findings emerge from other studies of such diverse occupations as sales personnel, college teachers, insurance underwriters, postal service carriers and assembly line workers.

Guidelines for Developing and Using Power

" "

Power does not kill; it permits suicide.

Earl Shorris
Manager and Writer

People respond in one of three ways when you use power:

- They may demonstrate commitment to your request and enthusiastically engage in the requisite behavior.

- They may comply; they go along with your request because they feel they have to, but they probably do not do anything beyond the minimum required.

- They may resist by failing to follow through or by fighting back.

Obviously, you need to understand how the various power bases can be used to generate commitment or, at the very least, willing compliance, rather than resistance to your requests.

Building and Using Referent Power

" "

The key to successful leadership is influence, not authority

Kenneth Blanchard
University of Massachusetts

You develop referent power when others on the project team respect and admire you personally. This source of power is almost solely determined by the way you treat people. Showing consideration for their needs and feelings, dealing with each person fairly and standing up for the group are ways to increase referent power. Face-to-face interaction with each individual is essential.

Another way you create referent power is by setting an example. You should intentionally set an example of what you expect and want from others. For example, if quality is important, you need to emphasize quality in all you do, from the products you produce to the correspondence you send out. If quality is important, make it the first item on the agenda of every team meeting and the first question you ask when reviewing individual progress.

Building and Using Expert Power

" "

One accurate measurement is worth a thousand expert opinions.

Grace Murray Hopper
1906-1992
Admiral, U.S. Navy

You cannot influence other people just because you are the technical expert. Others must recognize that you have the expertise and that you are a credible source of information and advice. Several factors help facilitate this process — for example, making sure that others are aware of your formal education, relevant work experience and significant accomplishments. You must also stay current and up-to-date. You cannot maintain an image of expertise unless you keep up with the developments in your field and remain professionally active.

Expert power can be undermined by relying too much on logic and rationale as persuasion tactics. One-way communication often leaves others feeling backed into a corner; trapped. Two-way communication, in which you uncover the feelings and concerns of others and deal with them in making persuasive arguments is much more effective.

Also, people react negatively to a manager who flaunts his or her greater expertise and experience. It is usually counterproductive to try to convince others by belittling their arguments or making them feel stupid. This will happen if you are perceived as treating their objections, concerns or suggestions as unimportant, trivial or insignificant. Recognizing the contributions of others, respecting their self-worth and incorporating, when possible, their ideas into action plans encourages their perception of your expertise — and your good sense.

Using Legitimate Power

" "

Control freaks don't grow good companies.

Jeffery A. Timmons
Babson College

Authority is exercised by making a legitimate request. You will encounter less resistance if you make it easy for others to comply with your request. The simplest way to do this is to make polite requests. These usually include the word "please." This is especially important for project personnel who are likely to be sensitive to status differences and authority relationships, for example, someone older or with more seniority than you or someone with multiple supervisors.

Another way to make it easy to go along is to explain the reasons behind the request. Others are more likely to go along with your requests if they see them as consistent with agreed-upon task objectives. It can be helpful to review the decision-making process with the team. Take the time to lead them through the process step by step. Show them why the decision was made and why other alternatives were rejected.

Finally, it is helpful when project personnel understand that your requests are within the scope of your authority. Linking requests with official documentation such as written rules, policies, contract provisions, and schedules is one way to do this. It is not sufficient to just say, "Trust me." It helps when people perceive that higher authority is on your side.

Using Reward Power

" "

The most important words in the English language:
5 most important words:
I am proud of you.
4 most important words:
What is your opinion?
3 most important words:
If you please.
2 most important words:
Thank you.
1 most important word:
You.

Anonymous

The most common way of using reward power is to offer tangible rewards to people if they go along with your requests. However, the ideal conditions for using reward power seldom exist. Most project leaders lack control over attractive tangible rewards. Project participants often have interdependent tasks that make if difficult to use individual incentives. In addition, objective indicators of performance are not available for many kinds of tasks and people's behavior is not often easily observable.

There are other problems with relying too heavily on rewards as a source of influence. You may win compliance but you are unlikely to win a person's heart or commitment. When people perform tasks to obtain a promised reward, they perceive their behavior as a means to an end. This may tempt them to take shortcuts and neglect less visible aspects of the task in order to complete the assignment and gain the reward. Few internal incentives are generated to motivate the individual to put forth any effort beyond what is required or to demonstrate any particular initiative in carrying out the task. Subsequently, their relationship with the project leader tends to be defined in purely economic terms. Special rewards come to be expected every time something new or unusual is required. Most managers run out of tangible goodies, especially as expectations escalate. In addition, using reward power can lead to resentment and resistance because people feel they are being manipulated by the contingent ("I'll do this if you do that") nature of the relationship.

Consequently, rather than using rewards as explicit incentives, effective project leaders use them more subtly to recognize and reinforce desired behavior. They focus on rewarding intrinsic needs like recognition, self-esteem and future opportunities for growth and challenge.

The use of reward power should supplement and strengthen your referent power base. Give rewards in a way that expresses your personal appreciation of efforts and accomplishments. People come to like people who repeatedly provide rewards in an acceptable manner. Interpersonal relationships are more satisfying when they are viewed as an expression of mutual friendship and loyalty rather than an impersonal economic exchange.

Using Coercive Power
** **

The emphasis in sound discipline must be on what's wrong, rather than who's to blame.

George S. Odiorne
1920-1992
American Educator and
Business Writer

Coercive power should be avoided except when absolutely necessary. Its use can create resentment and erode your personal power base. With coercion there is no chance of gaining commitment. Even willing compliance is difficult to achieve.

Coercion is most appropriate when it is used to stop behavior detrimental to the organization, for example, theft, sabotage, violation of safety rules or insubordination. Strategies of "positive discipline," rather than scaring people with threats or sample doses of punishment, are directed toward inducing others to assume responsibility for helping to resolve discipline problems. Here are some guidelines for using positive discipline:

- Let people know about rules and penalties for violations.

- Administer discipline consistently and promptly.

- Provide sufficient warning before resorting to punishment.

- Get the facts before using reprimands or punishments.

- Stay calm and avoid appearing hostile.

- Use appropriate punishments.

- Administer warnings and punishments in private.

Motivation

You can't motivate anyone to do anything. All you can do is create a set of circumstances in which they can motivate themselves. Motivation is purely internal. Abraham Maslow, a research psychologist, made a study of motivation and created a model of motivational factors that sums this up nicely. According to Maslow, we, as human beings, are all motivated by predictable, fundamental needs. These needs can be grouped into five categories that form a pyramid:

According to Maslow's theory, the most basic needs — food and water — are the basic drivers. Once these needs have been met, the Safety needs come into play. We are no longer content to be simply fed, we now work toward assuring our safety, through clothing, shelter, protection, etc.

Once the Safety needs have been met to our satisfaction, we move on to meeting our need for companionship — Affiliation. In modern society, these needs are met by family, friends and co-workers. After our Affiliation needs are sufficiently met, we move on to gratification of our own Egos. Ego needs include enhancing our sense of self-worth, status and gaining the respect of others.

The last step in Maslow's hierarchy is Self-actualization. In this stage, only after all other needs have been met, can we begin to realize our full potential as human beings.

Another element of Maslow's theory is that a "filled need is no longer a motivator." That is to say, once a need has been met, it no longer has the power to motivate us to do those things that led to its fulfillment. This is a key concept when trying to create motivational situations for people. The motivator must be something they want in order to be effective.

Most people in business are in the middle of Maslow's Hierarchy — in the Affiliation and Ego areas. Therefore, those things which fulfill Affiliation needs, such as cooperative relationships, involvement, participation, etc., and those things that satisfy Ego needs, such as praise, recognition, respect, etc., are the things that will provide the means for their motivation.

Leadership

Think of yourself as a leader rather than a manager. In general, managers "do things right" and leaders "do the right things." Leadership depends heavily on personal power. It is based on providing an inspiring vision of what needs to be done and providing the environment in which it can be accomplished.

It is important that among the sources of power, the central determinant is "in the eye of the beholder" — what counts is what others perceive. The way you handle yourself; your team member's interactions with you; your managerial style; etc., all influence people's perception of your power and hence the effect you have on their behavior.

What do others want from you? What do people expect from their leaders? Numerous studies, involving thousands of managers, have identified four personal characteristics that people admire, look for, and expect most from those they are willing to follow. Think about how you would measure up in the eyes of your project team.

What People Want From Their Leaders " "

Advice (From Kindergarten) For Managers:
- Share everything.
- Play fair.
- Don't hit people.
- Put things back where you found them.
- Clean up your own mess.
- Don't take things that aren't yours.
- Say you're sorry when you hurt somebody.
- Wash your hands before you eat.
- Flush.
- Warm cookies and cold milk are good for you.
- Live a balanced life — learn some and think some and draw and paint and sing and dance and play and work every day some.
- Take a nap every afternoon.
- When you go out into the world, watch out for traffic, hold hands and stick together.
- Be aware of wonder.

Robert Fulghum
Author

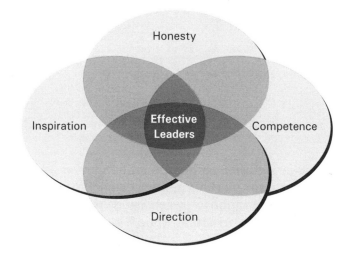

Honesty
The most frequently mentioned characteristic is honesty. People want a leader who is truthful with them and can be trusted. People judge your honesty by observing your behavior. Do you do what you say you are going to do, or not? Being honest is a game involving some risk. The leader must be the first to ante up.

Competence
The second most desired characteristic is competence. Before they will follow a request, people must believe that the person knows what he or she is doing. This does not necessarily involve functional or technical abilities. The specific kind of competence followers look for is affected by many factors, including position in the hierarchy and economic condition of the company. As a project leader, you must also be willing to demonstrate your ability to recognize the competence or expertise of those around you. In doing so, you demonstrate

your trust in others, not unlike the kind of trust you want others to feel toward you.

Direction

The third most frequently mentioned characteristic is a sense of direction. This trait should be a natural for project leaders. Leaders are expected to be forward-looking, to know where they are going and to be concerned about the future of the enterprise. People want to have a feeling for the destination the leader has in mind. The project leader's clarity about the target and the project objectives are akin to magnetic North on a compass. They pull the project team forward and keep it on course.

Inspiration

Finally, people expect their leaders to be inspiring. It is important that the project leader be seen as enthusiastic, energetic and positive about the project. Apple Computer manager Dave Patterson put it this way: "The leader is the evangelist for the dream."

Nora Watson, an editor, offers this view: "I think most people are looking for a calling, not a job. Most of us have jobs that are too small for our spirit." This is a reminder that you must help people on your project team find a greater sense of purpose and worth in their day-to-day life on the job. Effective project leaders inspire confidence in their project teams about the correctness of the project. They do this by their personal conviction and commitment to the project and by their actions.

Honesty, competence, being forward-looking and inspirational are the essence of credibility. When you are perceived as trustworthy, as knowing what you are talking about, as dynamic and sincere, and as having a sense of direction, others will see you as credible. When you have credibility, people are likely to comply with your requests and even more likely to demonstrate a sense of commitment in their follow-through regardless of the power source you tap into. Both you and others will feel empowered.

Over the years, there have been a number of major theories about leadership. We seem to be fascinated by the idea of "leaders" and are constantly seeking to understand what makes a good, or even a great, leader.

A Brief History of Leadership Theory

Over the last century, there have been a number of theories about leadership. The following is a brief tour of the four major theories.

The "Great Person" Theory

During the first half of the century it was generally accepted that some people had innate characteristics which caused them to be great leaders. The emphasis of this way of thinking about leadership was on the character of the leader. The theory also stated that these characteristics were "inborn" and that environmental factors could cause them to surface but could not instill them in someone in whom they did not already exist. Early studies into leadership behavior, however, demonstrated that only a small percentage of leaders fit this stereotype.

Theory "X" and Theory "Y"

66 99

Showing up is 80 percent of life.
Woody Allen
Actor, Director, Comedian

Two conflicting theories did battle in the middle of the century:

*   Theory X assumed that people dislike work, avoid responsibility, and require and desire direction and control. This was the prevailing theory at the time.

*   Theory Y assumed that people are internally motivated to achieve goals that they find meaningful, view work as being as natural as play, and can accept responsibility for providing their own direction.

*   Theory Y relied heavily on the work of Abraham Maslow on motivation (described earlier in this section). Theory Y stressed the need to find the motivators that would encourage the behaviors desired.

Task vs. Relationship Behavior

66 99

If you aren't fired with enthusiasm, you will be fired with enthusiasm.
Vince Lombardi
1913-1970
American Professional
Football Coach

Robert Blake and Jane Mouton developed their Managerial Grid theory to try to gain an understanding of why some individuals seem able to encourage and maintain high performance from their subordinates and peers and others do not. The Grid is a means of displaying the characteristics of leadership behavior that influence the behavior of others.

*   A leader with a high degree of emphasis on production, tasks and control was said to have a directive leadership style.

*   A leader with a high degree of emphasis on people development, relationships and supportive environment was said to have a participative or supportive leadership style.

The Grid is arranged on two axes: Concern for People (the vertical axis) and Concern for Production (the horizontal axis). An individual's placement on the grid is indicated by a pair of numbers indicating the strength of those two major concerns. The five number pairs shown on the Grid are the "archetypes" of the model.

The 1,1 in the lower left corner is called the Impoverished Manager. This individual exerts a minimum of effort to get required·work done in order to maintain his or her basic place in the organization.

The 9,1 in the lower right is the Authority/Obedience Manager. This individual believes that efficiency in operations results from arranging work in such a way that human elements interfere at a minimum.

The 5,5 in the middle is the Organization Man Manager. This individual believes that adequate organizational performance is possible through balancing the necessity to get out work with maintaining the morale of people at a satisfactory level.

The 1,9 in the upper left is the Country Club Manager. This individual is most concerned with providing satisfying relationships. This leads to a comfortable, friendly organization atmosphere and work tempo. The belief here is that if people are happy, acceptable work will get done.

The 9,9 in the upper right is the Team Manager. This individual believes that high-quality work is accomplished by committed people. They also believe that interdependence through a "common stake" in the organization's purpose leads to relationships of trust and respect.

Transactional (Situational) Leadership

" "

Different leadership situations require different leadership styles.

Paul Hersey and Kenneth Blanchard
Authors

According to Paul Hersey, "The most effective leader is one who can participate in a leadership transaction, and flex their own style to fit the requirements of the subordinate and situation."

The Situational Leadership model, first developed and presented by Paul Hersey and Ken Blanchard in 1969, has been updated to reflect new thinking about the relationship between the Style of the leader and the Development of the follower(s).

According to Blanchard and Hersey, three factors influence situational leadership:

• The leader's personal style as applied to a given situation.

• The situation in which the leadership transaction takes place.

• The development level of the follower in terms of his or her competence in relation to the situation at hand and their commitment which is defined as a combination of their confidence and motivation.

The descriptions of leadership styles are similar to those of Blake and Mouton in the Managerial Grid. They classify leadership behavior as either Directive or Supportive.

Directive behavior is characterized as structured, controlling, and supervisory in nature. Directive leadership is defined as the extent to which the leader:

- Engages in one-way communication.

- Spells out the follower(s) role.

- Tells the follower(s):

- What to do.

- Where to do it.

- When to do it.

- How to do it.

- Closely supervises performance.

Supportive (participative) behavior is characterized by praise, extensive uses of listening skills, and facilitation. Supportive behavior is defined as the extent to which the leader:

- Engages in two-way communication.

- Provides support and encouragement.

- Facilitates interaction.

- Involves the follower(s) in decision-making.

The situation is the second factor that impacts leadership style. This includes both the climate of the organization and broad personal development issues. Organizations have personalities. In some, participative behavior is not only encouraged, it is valued and rewarded. In others, directive behavior is the norm. This will impact a leader's ability to use a range of leadership styles to full effectiveness.

Within the larger organization, the ability and commitment of the work group affects the reaction to a particular situation, as does the type and degree of difficulty of the task at hand.

The third factor impacting leadership style is the needs of the follower. Things that will impact these needs include the follower's degree of:

- Need for independence.

- Need to participate in decisions.

- Identification with company goals.

- Personal commitment and motivation.

The Situational Leadership model goes on to describe four basic styles of leadership:

- Directing: Providing detailed instructions and watching to see that they are carried out.

- Coaching: Providing some instruction but mainly encouragement.

- Supporting: Providing mainly support.

- Delegating: Providing very little in the way of either instruction or support.

All of these factors are combined with the recognition that individuals will exhibit varying levels of competence and commitment in different situations. The two factors that the Situational Leadership model focuses on are:

- Competence, defined as the person's current skill, not their potential to develop a skill; and

- Commitment, defined as a combination of confidence; the person's self-assuredness, their belief that they can do the task well without supervision; and motivation, their interest and enthusiasm for doing the task.

As with leadership styles, Situational Leadership recognized four levels of follower development. Each of the levels requires a different leadership style.

If the development level is low competence but high commitment, the leader needs to provide direction.

If the development level shows some competence and a low level of commitment, the leader needs to provide both direction and support. This is the Coaching style.

If the development level demonstrates a high degree of competence but the commitment varies, the leader should provide support to bolster the commitment.

If the development level shows both high competence and high commitment, the leader needs to provide very little direction and support. This is the Delegation style.

The key point of the Situational Leadership model is that the leadership needs change from situation to situation, even though the same people may be involved. A simple example of this might be someone who is extremely competent in a particular area. As long as the work requires that skill, the leader can delegate the work with a high degree of confidence that it will be done well. This same individual, however, placed in a situation that requires other skills, knowledge and abilities may be on the bottom of the scale of development and require a highly directive leadership style.

An excellent book on this subject is: **Leadership and the One Minute Manager: Increasing Effectiveness Through Situational Leadership**, Kenneth Blanchard, et al, William Morrow & Co., 1985.

How Teams Grow and Change Over Time

> **" "**
>
> The whole object of organization is to get cooperation, to give each individual the benefit of the knowledge and all the experience of all individuals.
>
> **H.M. Barksdale**
> Management Executive Committee, DuPont

Maintaining the project team as a team; dealing with conflicts and problems between team members and between the team and other functional areas; and, ensuring that individual issues do not prevent progress on the project are also your responsibility.

The more technically-oriented a project, the greater the tendency to suppress people issues in favor of task issues. This is a very dangerous tendency. People are unique individuals, with individual wants and needs. They are not machines designed to perform tasks. The problems that destroy project teams are rarely technical in nature. They are usually emotionally based. Managing these issues is a significant part of your job.

The Team Growth Model

> **" "**
>
> The ratio of "We's" to "I's" is the best indicator of the development of a team.
>
> **Lewis D. Eigen**
> Executive Vice President
> University Research Corp.

Project teams are task teams. They exist to complete a task and, once that task is completed, they disband. This task-orientation can create some problems on the interpersonal level.

On-going teams, such as work groups or work teams, develop a style and procedures for dealing with interpersonal problems and conflicts that has as a primary element the continuing "health" of team members and of the team as a whole. Task teams frequently suppress interpersonal problems in favor of the task. This can lead to serious problems over the life of a project.

As the project leader, you have responsibilities for both sides of the team — task and interpersonal — and a model of how teams develop and change over time can be helpful in fulfilling these dual responsibilities.

There are several models of how groups develop over time. Most illustrate a series of stages through which groups pass on their way to maturity. This model is a combination of several and has been developed to show specifically how group development will impact a project team.

There are four stages in the model:

- Forming.

- Storming.

- Norming.

- Performing.

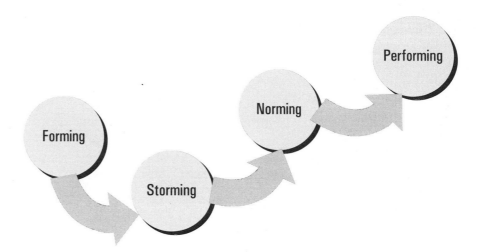

Each stage is characterized by specific behavioral characteristics. It is these characteristics which are the leader's clues about the stage of development of the group, and about how to help the group progress to the next stage in its development.

This model is a combination of elements from the work of George O. Charrier (Cog's Ladder), Bruce W. Tuckman (Tuckman's Model), Robert S. Blake and Jane S. Mouton (The Managerial Grid) and numerous other professionals concerned with the developmental sequence of small groups.

The development and testing of the various models has covered several decades and thousands of groups in virtually every culture. The models have proven to be valid regardless of the cultural surroundings and regardless of the purpose of the groups.

The model looks at two basic, and broad, behavioral dimensions: Task and personal interaction. Using these two dimensions, the model examines how individuals on the team and the team as a whole behave in each of the four stages of the model.

The task dimension is concerned with how individuals and teams focus and perform on the tasks of the group. It is concerned with the behaviors which direct the group toward achieving its goals and accomplishing its tasks in each stage.

The interaction dimension is concerned with how individuals and the team perform on the interpersonal level. It is concerned with the behaviors which are directed toward building and maintaining the group as a working unit and with achieving and maintaining member satisfaction.

Each stage has it's own distinctive behavior set. It is these behaviors which the project leader can affect by adjusting his or her own behavior to meet the leadership needs of the group.

Another characteristic of the stages is the range of participation by participants — at some stages, participation is fairly even by everyone; at others, the gap between high participators and low participators is very great.

We will examine each stage from both dimensions in the model and will then overlay a model of leader behavior which will help the group progress.

Participation Levels at Each Stage

" "

"Involvement" in this context differs from "commitment" in the same sense as the pig's and the chicken's roles in one's breakfast of ham and eggs. The chicken was involved — the pig was committed.

Anonymous

The following figure illustrates how the range of participation changes at each stage of the model. In the first stage, participation is fairly even by all participants. As the group moves into the second (Storming) stage, the gap between high and low levels of participation expands greatly with some individuals almost dropping out of the group and others taking a very strong role. As the group progresses through the last two stages, the range of participation narrows until the team reaches its optimum participation range.

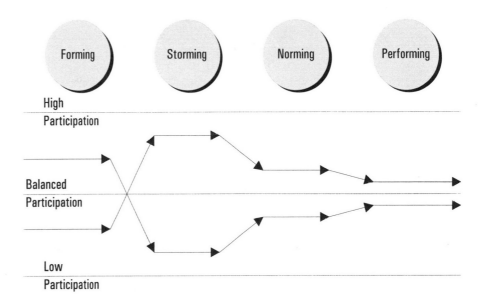

Forming

" "

We are, by nature, a tribal people.

Linda Ellerbee
Broadcast Journalist

In this first stage, the group is formed. It's mission is identified, major tasks and responsibilities are described. Members share personal and professional information. The team is dependent on the leader for direction.

Members try to determine "how I fit into the group." Members tend to be somewhat closed about feelings and don't share concerns or fears and, in many cases, do not share their questions about the task.

Typical behaviors in the Forming stage include:

• Members rely on stereotyping to help categorize each other: engineers, salespeople, bureaucrats, etc.

- Cliques are formed that will become important in later stages. Individuals with similar interests, professional credentials, etc., tend to group together.

- Hidden agenda items remain hidden. Individuals keep their personal desires for the group to themselves.

- The need for group approval is strong. This is a normal social need most people feel in new situations.

- The need for group identity is low. The group is not yet a team and has little sense of being a team.

- Members participate actively and conflict is usually absent. At this stage, people have little stake in the team and are more concerned with being accepted as individuals.

Another part of the Forming stage is the definition of why the group exists.

As the group moves past the initial "getting acquainted" activities, the reason for the group's existence becomes the focus. Members want to know the group's goals and objectives. Task-oriented groups spend more time at this stage while social groups spend very little.

- Cliques begin to wield influence. As the group's purpose is discussed, the stakes go up and sub-groups begin to jockey for positions of influence over the group's direction and purpose.

- Cliques flow and merge as they find common purpose. Alliances begin to form as the struggle for control escalates.

- Hidden agenda items begin to emerge as members try to verbalize group objectives that are most satisfying to themselves.

- Group identity is still low. At this point the group is a fragmented collection of individuals and small groups, not yet a team.

- The need for approval declines as members begin taking risks and displaying commitment.

- There is usually fairly active participation by all members.

The time spent in this phase varies widely. The easier the objectives are to define, the faster the group will move through this phase. When the purpose comes from outside the group (e.g., a task force with an assigned problem), the group will still discuss it in order to gain understanding and build commitment. The group also needs to know that the purpose agreed upon is important within the framework and nature of the group.

Storming

" "

A little rebellion now and then is a good thing.

Thomas Jefferson
1743-1826
Third President of the
United States

This is the most uncomfortable stage in the group's life. Task-oriented groups tend to try to ignore the interaction aspects of this stage. They try to subordinate everything to the task. Doing this can greatly prolong the time a group spends in this stage.

Members vie for influence. Conflicts occur. Confusion about roles and role boundaries may surface. Members jockey for power over the group's actions. Disagreements with the leader and with other members are common and will range from issues regarding goals, methods, resources and priorities to standards, values and personal style.

Group-building and maintenance roles are important. The harmonizer, the compromiser, the gatekeeper and the follower try to maintain a balance between the needs of individuals and the needs of the group.

Some of the characteristics of the Storming stage are:

- Activity is characterized by competition. Individuals and cliques compete for control with each other and with the leader. A member may try to rationalize his own position and to convince the group to take action he feels is appropriate. Other members are closed minded and accused of not listening.

- Conflict is at its highest level.

- A struggle for leadership occurs that involves all cliques or subgroups.

- Typical attempts to resolve the conflicts include voting, compromise and seeking arbitration from outside the group.

- Very little team spirit is present.

- Some members, who contributed willingly in the earlier phase, remain completely silent during this phase. Other members relish the opportunity to compete and attempt to dominate the group.

- Hidden agenda items begin to become public. As individuals and groups compete for control, their interests become more public.

- Feedback can be stinging. Criticism, which may have been completely absent in the earlier stage now emerges as a major force. It can get quite personal.

- Creative suggestions fall flat as they are seen as a bid for recognition and power. Very little constructive work is accomplished.

- Still no strong group identity. Instead, there may be several small groups, each with its own identity.

- The need for structure is strong. The leader must lead.

Some groups never get past this stage. They may still be able to fulfill their task, but data indicates that solutions arising out of Storming-stage activity are not optimum. They never satisfy all group members and are, at best, products of compromise.

Norming

" "

Make it clear that every-one is on the same team. Avoid practices that make it clear that some are on the first team and others are part of an-other.

Paul S. George
University of Florida

In the Norming stage, members are willing to change preconceived ideas or opinions on the basis of facts. Individuals actively ask questions and team spirit begins to build.

Resolution of conflicts in the Storming stage means agreements are being made — norms are being established. Members begin to feel increasingly comfortable with each other. The team begins to behave as a team. Expectations are clearer. Energy begins to focus almost exclusively on the task.

Some of the characteristics of the Norming stage are:

• An attitude change takes place. Members give up attempts to control and substitute active participation toward achieving group goals.

• Real progress toward group goals becomes evident as the energy of the group shifts from power struggles to task. Now the real work can be done.

• Leadership is shared. The person with the expertise to solve the problem at hand is the de facto leader.

• Group identity begins to become important. The members begin to think of themselves as part of a team.

• The range of participation narrows and a better balance is achieved.

• Conflict is dealt with as a group problem rather than a win-lose battle between individuals.

• The group is likely to use the talents of any individual who can contribute. Practical creativity is high and creative suggestions are solicited.

• An optimum solution or decision can result from Norming-stage interaction.

Exercises which enhance cooperation are very helpful in this stage. Those that enhance competition tend to disrupt and push the group back. At this stage it may be very difficult to integrate a new member.

Performing

66 99

When a team outgrows individual performance and learns team confidence, excellence becomes a reality.

Joe Paterno
Professional Football Coach

The overall feeling in this stage is that, "We don't always agree on everything but we do respect each other's views and we agree to disagree."

Norms become very strong and binding. Seldom are members distracted from the task.

Individually, and collectively, members are highly productive and are able to quickly resolve problems and disputes when they occur. Goals are achieved and the group makes rapid progress toward desired ends.

Some of the characteristics of the Performing phase are:

- High group morale and loyalty. The team has become more important than the individuals. Members tend to think of themselves in relation to the team.

- Relationships are empathetic. Individual members are more aware of, and therefore more willing to understand, each other's problems as they relate to the task.

- Need for group approval is absent since all members accept and approve of all others.

- Both individuality and creativity are high. Members actively support each other and contribute willingly to problem-solving efforts.

- Cliques are absent. The barriers between individuals, mostly based on areas of expertise, have been essentially removed.

- The group may create an identity symbol. Some companies are famous for their T-Shirt wardrobes. This is a function of Performing-stage activity.

- Participation is as evenly balanced as it will ever be. Not only is it balanced, it is as effective as it will get.

- The need for structure depends on whether the group is task or learning oriented. Learning groups at this stage have no need for formal structure. Task groups at this stage usually operate within a very loose, informal structure.

At this stage the group is strongly "closed." If a new member is introduced, the feelings of camaraderie and esprit will be destroyed since the group must regress to an earlier stage and then grow again into the performing stage, bringing the new member along with them.

Why Groups Move Up and Down the Model

Reasons prompting a group to move, or not to move, from one stage to another vary. For instance, the transition from Forming to Storming seems to occur when any single member desires it. He can simply say, "I think we should...." and the group will usually move to stage two.

Growing from Storming to Norming requires individuals to stop defending their own views and to risk the possibility of being wrong. Norming demands some humility.

The step from Norming to Performing demands that a member trust himself and other group members. And to trust is to risk a breach of that trust.

Adding a new member, or members, seems to be the most common reason for a group to go backward on the model. This is especially true if the group is in the Norming or Performing stages. The addition of a new member during these stages disrupts the "group personality." The new member has not shared the group experiences that led them to these stages. As a result, the group must revert to an earlier phase and assist the new member, or members, to develop along with the group. An enthusiastic new member, one who has a stake in the group's purpose, can proceed through the steps fairly rapidly. An opinionated new member, one with a strong hidden agenda, can slow the process considerably.

One of the most beneficial activities for the group occurs in the first two stages: Development of a shared goal. If the purpose the group develops is clear and motivating, the group will use the purpose as a touchstone in all subsequent stages as a means of focusing group activity. The Storming stage will be resolved when the entire group has reconciled its various hidden agendas and personal needs with the group's stated purpose. The Norming stage will focus on working toward achieving that purpose in small and large ways. The Performing stage will focus on the group's successes and the personal and group sense of achievement and worth.

The ability to listen has been found to be the most important trait in helping groups move from Storming to Norming. In some cases, where the group as a whole desired to relate in the Norming stage while some members stayed rooted in the Storming stage, groups have been observed to reject those members. On the other hand, the transition from Storming to Norming can be permanently blocked by a strong member or their clique.

The transition from Norming to Performing seems to require unanimous agreement among group members.

Group cohesiveness seems to depend on how well the group members can relate in the same phase at the same time. A group will proceed through the four stages only as far as its individual members are willing to grow. Each member must be willing to give up something at each step in order to make the move to the next step.

To grow from Forming to Storming, for example, each member must relinquish the comfort of non-threatening topics and risk the possibility of conflict. Moving into the Storming stage requires members to put aside a continued discussion of the group's purpose and commit to a purpose with which they may not totally agree. They must also risk personal attacks which will occur in the Storming stage.

Leadership Responsibilities at Each Stage

In order to assist the team to move from one stage to the next, the leader must focus on certain mixes of behavior at each stage. As the team moves through the various stages of the model, the leader should keep focused on where the group should be headed — not on where they've been.

In the first two stages, the team will expend a great deal of energy on the task aspects of relationships and therefore the leader should focus on the interaction aspects.

In the last two stages, the team will be more interactive and will require less assistance on that front. The leader should keep a "weather eye" on the interactions but should help keep the team focused on its tasks.

Forming

During the Forming stage, the leadership style is primarily directive. Not in the sense of being a dictator but more in the sense of providing a set of guidelines.

- Provide time and a structure in which the group can get acquainted and share personal and technical information.

- Introduce the task and guide the discussion about how it should be done.

- Be ready to clarify misconceptions about the task and to lay out your vision of the roles, responsibilities and division of the overall project into specific tasks.

- Constantly test for agreement as the discussion progresses. Begin to build the parts of the common vision.

- Seek input from individuals and groups about how they view their roles, their contribution and their estimates about the time and resources necessary to complete their activities.

- Restate agreements, check for hesitation or uncertainty.

Forming – Common Problems

Problem:

- Trust level is low, members are too quiet, fail to share or ask questions.

Leader actions:

• Allow extra time for socializing; schedule pre-meeting meetings; talk with members individually; structure sharing activities; model the desired behavior.

Problem:

• Members fail to fully understand the mission, task, role relationships, and leader expectations, and don't ask questions about them.

Leader actions:

• Put this information in writing; display it; act as a teacher; meet one-on-one to solicit reactions and questions.

Storming During the Storming stage, the leadership style is primarily one of coaching. You can't smother the conflict but you can help the team work it out.

First of all, expect Storming to occur. It is a perfectly natural part of a group's development. One of the reasons primarily social groups rarely accomplish much of real worth in terms of tasks is that they try to avoid the "unpleasantness" of this stage. As a result, they rarely make it to the next, more productive stages.

Storming is the group's "de-bugging" mechanism. One of the best things you, as a leader, can do is to reassure the team that this is a natural part of becoming a high-performance team.

• Work on bringing the reasons for conflict to the surface. Whether this is done in the context of the group or individually with members is the leader's choice. Be aware that some people simply cannot deal with conflict publicly.

• Always go for the underlying issue in a conflict, not the surface symptoms.

Storming – Common Problems

Problem:

• Members are fearful of conflict and resist sharing openly, yet hidden conflicts and agendas block the group.

Leader actions:

• Work individually with members to deal with reasons for conflict. Raise issues on agendas: "Fuzzy role boundaries cause confusion."

Problem:

- Highly-charged emotional confrontations make the group very tense and uncomfortable; negative feelings block task achievement.

Leader actions:

- Try to separate the emotional and the substantive conflict issues. Act as a "third party" to mediate disputes. Move the discussion into the negotiation arena and search for workable solutions.

Norming During the Norming stage the leadership role is primarily that of a developer. The individuals and work groups have resolved the majority of their interaction problems. Now they need help getting the work done.

- Help the team stay focused on the task. The project goal statement will help with this as will other project control tools.

- Formalize the agreements between individuals and groups which will assist in accomplishing their parts of the task.

- Help resolve task-related problems. Technical issues, resource issues, schedules and alternative approaches to problems are the focus of the group's energy. Provide the assistance needed to resolve them.

- Barrier-bashing is the project leader's main job. The team is performing well on the task, your job is to get the roadblocks down so they can continue.

Norming – Common Problems

Problem:

- A new member is introduced into the team and upsets the norms.

Leader actions:

- Treat this situation as normal and expected. Help the new member to find his or her place and assist members to adjust roles and responsibilities as needed.

Special note: The introduction of a new member is the most common reason for disruption in a team. The leader must take an active role in integrating the new member into the team.

Performing   The leadership style for the Performing stage is that of a consultant. The leader steps in when asked or when a problem becomes evident.

- Watch for breakdowns in spirit, goal clarity and cohesion. These are the areas where "burnout" is most likely to appear first. The more task-driven the individuals, the more likely some burnout symptoms will appear.

- Keep the team "tuned and energized." A little cheerleading never hurts. In this stage, it is a major leader activity.

- Protect the team from, or help them deal with, distractions that originate from outside and hinder performance. At this stage, much of the project leader's time is spent running ahead of the team getting things out of their way.

Performing – Common Problems

Problem:

- Performance begins to lag due to fatigue and burnout.

Leader actions:

- Ease off on expectations a bit. Provide breaks from the routine such as an off-site event, or time off. Encourage the use of available time off. In smaller ways, break up the routine with short impromptu gatherings.

Problem:

- A major change in the larger environment upsets resources or timelines.

Leader actions:

- Collect and share accurate information to dispel rumors. Identify how the change will affect the work of the group. Accept members' negative feelings about the change to provide for some catharsis. Re-assess the goals and timelines and make adjustments as required.

Negotiation

" "

Perfectionists make poor negotiators. If you hold out for the perfect deal, you'll likely never close, you'll almost always have to leave something on the table.

Lewis D. Eigen
Executive Vice President,
University Research Corp

Negotiation skills are a necessary part of the tool kit of any successful project leader. You will negotiate for resources, assistance, expertise, time, almost everything connected with your project. The following is adapted from the best book on Negotiation I have ever found: **Getting to Yes: Negotiating Agreement Without Giving In**, by Roger Fisher and William Ury, Penguin Books, 1981.

Negotiation is a two-way process. It usually involves a significant amount of give-and-take. When difficulties arise, you can try to reach an agreement in several ways: You can give in to the other person; you can try to smooth over the disagreement; you can try to suppress the points of contention; you can try splitting the difference; you can try arguing; you can try persuading; or, you can try to find common ground on which to bargain and negotiate differences.

As a project leader, the problem of persuading another person or department to adopt your point of view or to go along with your requests for support is complicated by the fact that you may lack the "power of the hierarchy." You may lack formal authority. You may not be the other person's boss, and you may not have the right to command or to give orders that others are expected to follow.

One method for gaining acceptance of your viewpoint is to provide a sound rationale for your position. This is the power of intellect or expertise. People generally go along with a person who is perceived as being an expert in the area under discussion. Expressing expertise consists of communicating your rationale with reason and logic. Within functional areas, this tactic may prove useful, but project leaders usually operate in more than one functional area. It is difficult to have (or to be perceived as having) expertise across many disciplines. You should, however, try to be conversant across functional areas — you need to have some fundamental knowledge of each area with which you must work. Effective project leaders are perceived by people in each functional area as knowing something about their discipline and appreciating their point of view.

The problem with trying to rely on logic and reason in managing differences is that reason does not always prevail. Logic, data and reason do not always point to a clear solution agreeable to everyone. Competing points of view cannot be resolved by logic when each is based on a sound rationale. An example might be people from very different technical backgrounds (for example computer programming and marketing, or financial analysis and production) who must arrive at a common course of action. The backgrounds they bring to the discussion are so divergent that satisfaction on common ground is very difficult.

Facts, Goals, Methods, Values

" "

Deep-seated preferences
cannot be argued about.
Oliver Wendell Holmes, Jr.
1841-1935
U.S. Supreme Court Justice

Most negotiations revolve around one or more of the following issues:

- Facts.

- Goals.

- Methods.

- Values.

As you move down this list, the difficulty of reaching an agreement increases until you get to the issue of Values, where disagreements can rarely be resolved.

- Facts are verifiable. They can be examined, tested and agreed upon from sound evidence. Agreeing about the facts of a situation is not usually very difficult. If everyone agrees with the premise used to develop the facts, agreement should be easy. For example, if everyone agrees that marketing's research shows that the company's market share is indeed lower than it was last year at this time, you have agreement on the fact.

- Goals are a little rougher. If the goal being negotiated is based on facts, the task is much simpler. Getting agreement about a goal usually requires that everyone agree that the goal is worth achieving, and commit to it. Using the same example as above, if everyone agrees that market share is down, it is probably not too much of a stretch to gain agreement about a goal to increase market share.

- The majority of negotiations around projects center on methods — the "how" of the project. For every goal there are likely to be as many ideas about how to reach it as there are people involved. Logic, practicality, simplicity, expense, etc., are all things that must be considered when seeking agreement about methods. Still sticking with the market share example, several methods might achieve the goal of increasing market share. The company could lower prices. They could increase advertising. They could change marketing strategies to open new markets. They could introduce new products into existing markets. They could...you get the picture.

- Values are generally not negotiable. Values are things that are so much a part of us that we wouldn't change them even if we could. People's personal values do not often come into conflict with a project but, if they do, trying to negotiate an agreement that results in someone changing, or compromising, a personal value will most likely end with no resolution and can have other negative consequences. Most people don't like having their values questioned. If you encounter a value-based issue, try to find some way around it without having to confront the individual. One example of a potential values conflict could be the issue of overtime. If the project is running behind schedule and there is a need to get back on track, one option might be to work two or three Saturdays and a few late evenings. For many, this is not a problem, particularly if they are compensated for the extra time. However, some people simply do not see this as a viable alternative. Their value system places more importance on time with family than time at work. The occasional late evening or partial Saturday is not a problem. However, a series of them begins to raise the specter of conflict with deeply held values that some people are unwilling to compromise.

Four Tactics for Building Agreement

" "

The old idea of a good bargain was a transaction in which one man got the better of another. The new idea of a good contract is a transaction which is good for both parties.

Louis D. Brandies
U.S. Supreme Court Justice

According to Fisher and Ury, there are four tactics which can help build agreements in which all parties participate:

1. Create a common ground.

2. Enlarge areas of agreement.

3. Gather information.

4. Focus on issues, not personalities.

Create a Common Ground

Forming a strong foundation is the most important step in building any lasting agreement. What do you and the other person already have in common? On what do you already agree? What are you both trying to accomplish? In the case of projects, ideally the project goal should sum up the common ground.

You want to keep in mind what you have in common, not those things on which you disagree. Pushing people apart at the beginning of a dialogue rarely helps build an atmosphere of cooperation. Agreeing on a common ground highlights the important interdependencies. "When my success depends on your success, and vice versa, we are both more likely to work through our differences than when our successes are independent."

This is just one more reason why you should work so hard at the beginning of the project — in the planning phase — to involve all the affected parties in determining the project's goal and creating a schedule that underscores the critical interdependencies.

Enlarge Areas of Agreement

The second step is to build on and expand the common ground you have established. You have to move out of "selling your idea," or "if I can only convince them" mode. If possible, you should try to find some benefit for the other person if they will agree with your proposal. In many cases, this can be as simple as "With your help, the project will get done. Without it, it won't." If the project itself is important to the person or to the company in general, this is often sufficient benefit. In other cases, the benefit may need to be more personal or more specific.

In the process of expanding on common ground, time is required to allow each person to get their ideas on the table. Too often, participants in a conflict get involved in attacking and defending and devote almost no time to listening and trying to build an agreement. The agreement-building process is facilitated when we:

•   Allow each person to state his or her position without interruption.

•   Allow a brief period of time for questions of clarification only.

•   Ask "How can we each get what we want?"

When arguing is leading nowhere, the skilled negotiator will switch to statements of possible exchange: "If you would be willing to do X, I would be willing to do Y." This transforms an argument into a discussion and a potential deadlock into a settlement.

Gather Information

Working through fundamental issues, such as "Who is involved or concerned with this issue?," "Who can help resolve the conflict?," and "Is all the information needed to resolve the conflict available?," helps to create a working foundation for discussion. If you cannot agree which parties are really involved or concerned with the issue, some important points of view may not be represented in the negotiations. The needs of these people will not be represented in the proposed solutions and you will have the beginnings of another conflict.

The issue of the information needed to resolve the conflict is a critical one. If insufficient or inaccurate information is used to reach an agreement, the agreement is flawed from the outset. Be sure to have all the available information when you are in a negotiation situation. This can be the key to success.

You may find yourself in a conflict over a problem, for example a scheduling conflict, which you and the other person cannot resolve. When you have actually reach a dead end, don't continue to try to batter an agreement out of someone. This is the good news about working on projects inside an organization: You can usually find someone higher in the organization to make the decision if necessary. When you are really stuck — when you and the other party simply can't come to an agreement that will resolve the problem — try for an agreement to take it to the next level.

Focus on Issues, Not Personalities

It is crucial to depersonalize conflict. When someone feels they must defend themselves from personal attack, they typically react with one of the two sides of what psychologists call the "fight or flight" response:

- They fight back, which only escalates the disagreement and makes finding common ground much more difficult. In a fight, the other person's energies are devoted to getting back at you, not on solving the problem.

- They flee and you don't get people to commit their energies to problem-solving. Although they may agree on an action, they will have no real commitment to follow through once you are out of sight.

One of the best ways to focus on issues and not on personalities is to be future-oriented. "What are we going to do about this?" rather than "Why can't you be more reasonable?" or "Who got us into this mess?" By being future-oriented you emphasize building agreement on a future action rather than on blaming each other for past problems. This does not mean you don't want to explore the past for insights into the causes of the problem, but emphasizing the past often leads to one person having to defend his or her actions, or blame and scapegoat someone else. "What are we going to do to ensure that this doesn't happen again?" is a statement of allies against a problem, not against each other.

Negotiation Techniques

Successful project leaders are effective negotiators. Much has been written about how successful negotiators behave — what they do and what they try to avoid doing as they build agreements between people. Management consultant Clifford Bolster reports in his studies that technically trained managers frequently discover, much to their discomfort, that they rely too heavily on reasoning and logic in trying to get others to do what they want. He observes, "Negotiation is a process that may be used when logical reasoning has run its course, and represents a critical skill for the technical manager today."

The objective of negotiation is to reach an agreement that satisfies both parties. Satisfaction is an emotional, not a logical, experience. Negotiation is not an optimal, dispassionate problem-solving experience where analysis and reasoning are the only skills needed to determine the cause of the problem and to reach the solution with the highest probability of solving the problem.

The best solution in negotiations is the one that satisfies both parties and results in committed follow-through on the solution. This does not mean that analytical skills are not needed in negotiation, just that they are not paramount. They take up time and get in the way of efforts that could be devoted to building an agreement.

In order to be a skilled negotiator, each of the following techniques should be part of your tool kit:

- Be direct. Act rather than react. Be a problem finder. Be clear about your interests and needs.

- Label behavior. For clarity, make prefacing remarks during the negotiation. "What I'd like to do is propose..." and "May I make the suggestion that..." reduces ambiguity about your intentions. If you do this, you are unlikely to be accused of making a "power play."

- Avoid argument. Argument during the negotiation dilutes the process and gets people off the track of searching for and building agreements. Remember, arguments are emotional. They are seldom resolved with logic and facts.

- Be aware of the limitations of logic. Rather than relying too heavily on logic and reason, try this attitude: "What seems reasonable to you is reasonable to me." Exchange statements play a pivotal role in this process. Sensitivity to others' perceptions is vital.

- Know what you want and ask for it. If you don't know what you want, you can't ask for it. If you don't ask for it, you're not likely to get it. Nobody can read your mind, nor can you read anyone else's mind. Assertive expressions of needs, interests and possible exchanges move the negotiations along.

- Repeat expectations firmly. Persist in stating expectations, wants and needs and in not letting the other person off too easily or making it easy for them to say no. By building on common ground, make it possible for the other person to say yes.

- Don't justify. Too often, justification seems like rationalization and clutching at straws. Rather than justify defensively, make firm assertions backed by facts when appropriate.

- Avoid "irritants." Words and phrases like "Anyone could see that...," "It's always been done this way...," "My generous offer...," and the like push the other party into a corner where their only options are "fight or flight." Keep the discussion focused on the issues not on personalities.

- Create alternative solutions. Understand that both your own interests and those of the other person can probably be satisfied by more than one solution. Imagination is required both to understand and to use what you have that the other person wants or needs, and vice versa. Often this entails numerous "What if" statements. Inflate trial balloons and float them for possible agreement.

By effectively managing and negotiating disagreements, you will achieve positive outcomes from the inevitable differences and conflicts which arise in project management. You can get the job done most effectively when you build agreements that vitalize participants. Conflict, in and of itself, is not a bad thing. Conflict creates energy that is vital to managing projects from inception to completion. It is when conflict is allowed to get out of control or when it begins to get into the realm of personalities that it becomes a problem. Anticipating the sources of conflict and understanding the ebb and flow of conflicts in a project environment will increase your ability to harness this energy. Paradoxically, finding — or, if necessary, creating — areas of agreement is an important starting place for negotiating differences.

Communication

" "

Communication is not just words, paint on canvas, math symbols or the equations and models of scientists: It is the interrelation of human beings trying to escape loneliness, trying to share experience, trying to implant ideas.

William M. Narsteller
Advertising Executive

Of all the skills a project leader needs to be effective, communication is one of the most important. Without good, two-way communication in and around the project, trouble is almost guaranteed.

Most of the material in this section deals with face-to-face, verbal, interpersonal communication between the project leader and project team members and stakeholders in the project community. There is, however, a new wrinkle in the communication matrix in many organizations — telecommunication technology.

In the broadest sense, this technology falls into two categories: Voice and text.

In the voice category we have two wonderful inventions:

- Voice mail.

- Automated routing systems.

Most of us have played "phone tag" with someone. You call and leave a message; they return your call and leave a message; you return the call and leave a message; they return your message; your machine calls their machine; your machines strike up a relationship and elope.

Voice mail, like most of the telecommunication technologies is great if it is used properly. If messages are returned in a timely manner; if enough information is left in the message to allow for a return message that answers the question; if you don't get stuck in a phone tag loop.

Automated routing systems are handy if the instructions on their use are well crafted or if you know how to navigate the system. It is also nice if there is an "escape" function that allows you to get out of the system and talk to a person.

Of these two technologies, voice mail is most likely to have an impact on communication on a project. The need to interface with project team members on a frequent basis makes the use of voice mail likely. You, as the project leader are likely to be the initiator of most of this communication and, as such, you should know how to use the system effectively. Some hints include:

- Be specific in your message. Don't ramble.

- If you are asking a question, specify what you require as a response and ask that the person contact you (or your voice mail system) with the answer. Attach a time-frame to your request.

- Specify when you will be available for a return call.

- If you are passing on information, be clear and concise.

- When trying to schedule a meeting, give alternative dates and times and ask that the return message specify which alternative will work.

In the text category, we have two major technologies:

- Fax.

- Electronic Mail (E-Mail).

Fax technology has come a long way from its beginnings. Fax modems are now included in most personal computer systems. The quality of the faxed document has improved significantly from the early days.

Faxing information has become common-place and can be an excellent way to transmit printed (either text or images) material very quickly from one site to another. The fax, however, is not a truly interactive device. Most of its uses center around sending information in one direction for review or instruction. There is little, if any personal contact between the parties.

E-Mail, on the other hand, has enjoyed an explosion of use in the last few years. Like many technologies before it (including the fax) it has begun to generate its own work. What was once perfectly acceptable to send by "snail mail" (the U.S. Post Office) now must be transmitted instantaneously by E-Mail. The capability to send the same message to a large number of people with the press of a button has added to the general overuse of this technology. Anyone with E-Mail capabilities will soon find themselves buried in messages, most of which they don't really need.

The amount of time that can be eaten up by going through one day's accumulated E-Mail can be frightening. Many people are so overwhelmed by the load, they simply delete messages that don't appear important without reading them. Others actually read everything that comes through and use up valuable time that could be put to better use.

If you must use E-Mail to communicate about your project, follow some of these simple rules to increase its effectiveness:

- Use E-Mail only when it is the best choice for the communication. If a phone call would really be better, make the call.

- Clearly identify the subject of the message in the header.

- Send E-Mail only to those people who need to see the message. Don't use the "Send To Complete List" command for everything.

- Keep the message short and to the point.

- If a response is required, be specific about what you need and when you need it.

One use of E-Mail that is a real boon to project management is the ability to use it to distribute project status reports, meeting minutes and other project-wide information. It is also useful for keeping stakeholders (other than team members) updated on progress.

Interpersonal Communication

Have you sometimes wondered why it seems so difficult to communicate with some people? And why at other times you instantaneously hit it off with someone you have just met? There seems to be a basis of understanding that is more than could be explained by a common background of related professions.

Or perhaps you've been surprised by an abrupt breakdown in understanding when talking to a friend or business associate. You may have spent several minutes presenting what you see as relevant information — background material, pertinent facts, logical opinions, various options, etc. Your friend and associate has been growing progressively more restless. Then you decide to tell him how it feels and, suddenly you have instant communication.

What accounts for this change? And why do we seem to relate better with some people than with others?

The Four Basic Communication Styles

" "

Eloquence is the power to translate a truth into language perfectly intelligible to the person to whom you speak.

Ralph Waldo Emerson
1803-1882
American Essayist and Poet

The secret was unlocked by Carl Jung, a Swiss psychoanalyst, in a monumental work, **Psychological Types**, written in the 1920's but not translated in its entirety and published in the U.S. until 1974.

What really accounts for personality differences, Jung said, is that every individual develops a primacy in one of four major behavioral functions:

- Intuiting: Speculating, imagining, envisioning, daydreaming, creating, innovating.

- Thinking: Rationally deducting, analyzing, ordering facts, identifying and weighing options, reflecting.

- Feeling: Empathizing, perceiving, associating, remembering, relating.

- Sensing: Acting — doing, relying on sensory data, combating — competing, striving for results, living in the here and now.

Behavior patterns, Jung claimed, are reflected by infants during their first days of life. Study young children, he said, truly observe them and you will discover that they process experience on different primary channels. Jung contended that children in elementary school could be validly classified as intuitors, thinkers, feelers, and sensors.

The intuitor child sits alone, apparently daydreaming. In reality, the child is forming global concepts, integrating experience in a constant quest to determine the why of things. Knowing something because the teacher says it's true is not sufficient. They must discover why a thing is true. In the absence of such discovery, they will summarily reject your premise.

The thinker child prides himself or herself on being correct. They demonstrate a structured and systematic approach to learning. They gather facts, not ideas. Their concern is to systematize, to collect and infer but not to dream. Their approach is information-centered.

The feeler child responds to mood, their own as well as the emotions of others. They learn through their emotions. They are empathetic, sentimental. They demonstrate keen interpersonal radar. Whether or not they engage in an activity with true commitment depends upon its perceived meaning in terms of past experience, not future possibilities or book-learned facts. Their touchstone of reality is meaningful memories.

The sensor child is the doer, the fast mover, the restless jack-in-the box, the learner who must grab the rock or the doll in their own hands to know its reality; the child who is sent to the principal's office today and who emerges as the corporate president of one of Fortune's 500 tomorrow. They dissipate anxiety through action, they know by doing — not by imagining, thinking, or feeling.

So what does all this have to do with the adult in today's workplace? Many of us are really only larger versions of the children we once were. We carry over to adult life most of the basic habits and practices of our early years. According to Jung's theories, the following can be considered true and valid:

- Everyone of us uses a blend of the four behavioral styles. No one is a walking "pure style" or cardboard creature.

- Despite using a blend or style-mix, each person relies most heavily on a primary or dominant style or styles.

- An individual's weaknesses, or areas of key behavioral difficulty, often represent an over-extension of their strengths.

- An individual's style is reflected in their behavior and is therefore observable and identifiable.

And now Jung's theories have been translated into action terms, making the theory "see-able" and "do-able." If people do use these four main styles to process information (receive) and to broadcast information (send), then it follows that one of the primary functions of these styles is to serve as communication channels.

No style should be considered good or bad. No one style is more "right" or "wrong" than another. The communicating styles we have developed over the years have little to do with intellectual abilities, aptitudes, performance, or concerns with mental health or illness. You use four main channels of communication; so do I. So does every boss and every subordinate, every salesman and every customer, every husband and every wife, every teacher and every pupil.

Transactional analysis suggests that if you and I are communicating in our everyday modes, we will be engaged in adult-to-adult communication, or a parallel transaction. Not necessarily so.

Why? If you are a primary sensor you want to know immediately what I am proposing, what the upshot or bottom line is that I'm suggesting.

If I'm a primary thinker, and I want you to know all the facts and insist on giving you a long-detailed rundown on my fact-finding and historical review of the situation, we are not effectively communicating in parallel.

When and How to Use the Various Styles
" "

How well we communicate is determined not by how well we say things but by how well we are understood.

Andrew S. Grove
CEO, Intel Corp.

It is very difficult to have a successful communication experience if I'm trying to speak to you on one channel and you are receiving on another. The whole process is further complicated by the fact that often we change our channels when we perceive ourselves to be in stressful conditions. For example, the normally fast-moving, hard-charging sensor may become, under stress, a conservative, cautious, weighing thinker.

Individuals can learn to read their communicating styles more accurately, and to read and assess the styles of the individuals with whom they do business on a daily basis. Once they accept this concept and relate it to increased personal awareness, it's time to learn to style-flex. Style-flexing means communicating with another individual on their primary channel rather than communicating with all people as though they were all, say, primary thinkers. Is it really possible? Absolutely. Is it easy? Certainly not.

Jung indicated that individuals rarely outgrow or discard their primary styles. In other words, a person's communicating style tends to be very stable through time. What we can do, however, is learn to "flex" our communication styles to better match with those of the person with whom we are trying to communicate.

Style-Flexing   It would be difficult, if not impossible, for you or me, even as a full time professional, to style-flex continuously over a 24-hour period. That is, if you're primarily a thinker, it would be unrealistic to expect you to be able to communicate effectively as a feeler for an entire day. But most transactions are much shorter in duration. How long is an average workplace interaction? Fifteen minutes? How about an average meeting — an hour? How long is a typical boss-subordinate performance review session — an hour or two? Most people can, with practice, learn to style-flex for limited periods of time.

And style-flexing is, in itself, not the only key. Sometimes just asking a person the "right question" can thaw a difficult communication transaction.

- To an intuitor: "How do you feel about the basic concept underlying this proposal?"

- To a thinker: "Based on your own analysis, how would you evaluate the relevance of the facts I've presented?"

- To a feeler: "I've given this a lot of consideration but I'd like to know how you feel we're tracking."

- To a sensor: "I hope I haven't bored you; what's your reaction to the main point here?"

If you take the time and trouble to learn the techniques presented here and to apply them by style-flexing, will people regard you as a phoney? That's a common fear, but experience proves quite the contrary. People will say, "Now you're on my wave length!," or "I appreciate your being open enough to share some of your doubts and apprehensions," or "Thanks for boiling it down and respecting the fact that I really don't have a lot of time to spend on this."

Notes on the Four Communication Styles

So, who are these people? How do you spot them in a group? How does all this relate to project management?

Let's take the last question first. Projects are completed by people. Without the active participation of people working on your project, it won't get done. As a project leader, you need to be able to communicate effectively with all the people connected with, or impacted by your project. The following notes should help you to identify the primary styles of most of the people with whom you will interact. And, knowing that, you should be able to more effectively communicate with them.

One special note: One of the things that Jung discovered in his research was that, for most of us, our communication weaknesses are frequently over-extensions of the strengths of our primary style. These will be identified in the notes below.

The Intuitor   The Intuitor is the big-picture thinker of the group. Intuitors deal very well with abstract concepts and theories. They tend to be quite intuitive and can often make surprising connections between seemingly unconnected ideas. Intuitors are very good at linking the various parts into a single whole. Their time-orientation is toward the future.

On projects, Intuitors are the keeper of the vision. They understand the long-range implications of the work being done and can help keep the team focused on the goal. Their ability to deal with large concepts makes them valuable in planning.

The Intuitor's weakness, as Jung pointed out, is often an over-extension of the very thing that makes them what they are: When they get too deeply into the conceptual and abstract, they can simply disconnect from reality. They can drift off, thinking lofty thoughts and not get anything of practical value done.

When communicating with an Intuitor, keep these things in mind: Allow enough time. Start with an overview and explain where you want to go with your suggestion. Show that your ideas are innovative, unique, original, unusual, creative, etc. Conceptualize your ideas and tie them into overall concepts. Show the impact on the future.

The Thinker   Where the Intuitor is the big-picture person, the Thinker is into the details. Thinkers tend to like structure and order. They like facts, backed up with analysis and logic. They tend to be somewhat formal in their dealings with others. They do not cope well with "cloudy, blue-sky pictures." Thinkers do not usually make hasty decisions. They think things through very thoroughly and weigh all the options before deciding on a course of action. Their logic is a source of pride. They are meticulous and organized. Their time-orientation is all three; past, present, and future, but from a fact-based point of view.

On projects, Thinkers are the keepers of the details and records. They focus on the small things that go into the overall work. They are aware of the necessity for good records and careful planning.

Once again, their greatest potential weakness is an over-extension of their strength. Taken too far, their love of details can be seen as nit-picking. If allowed to get out of hand, their need for comprehensive plans and careful analysis can be seen as the "paralysis of analysis" that keeps the planning going long after the time has come to get the work started.

When communicating with a Thinker, keep these things in mind: Gather your facts and line up your sources. Get organized. Provide the Thinker with enough facts that they will come to the same conclusion you did. Have some alternatives. Organize your presentation — use a systematic progression. Use the scientific method. Be prompt. Be factual and objective, avoid emotion. Be precise and exact, avoid ambiguity.

The Feeler Feelers tend more toward the interpersonal aspects of life and less toward its mundane side. Feelers are very people-oriented. They tend toward informality and close relationships. Their interpersonal skills are naturally quite good and they use them to good advantage when dealing with others. They are empathic by nature and can usually "read" the emotional state of a group very accurately. Because their time-orientation is the past, Feelers are likely to be into nostalgia and memorabilia.

On projects, Feelers can help hold the group together. Their natural abilities with people make them invaluable in dealing with the emotional ups and downs of most projects. They can also contribute relevant past experiences and a good sense of the human impacts of the project.

The Feeler's potential weakness lies in carrying their natural affinity for people to extremes. They are so good at "seeing the other person's point of view" that they may not be able to stand up for an unfavorable position. Decisions with negative human impacts can be very difficult for a Feeler.

When communicating with a Feeler, keep these things in mind: Be informal, become acquainted with small talk. Allow enough time for the chit chat. You can meet with them over lunch or in an informal atmosphere. Personalize your presentation, and show its impact on people. Capitalize on tradition and past practices.

The Sensor The Sensor is the "doer" of the group. Sensors are action-oriented, hard working and can handle a lot of work. The saying, "If you want a job done, give it to a busy person," seems made to describe the Sensor. They deal with the world through all their senses and they tend to take large bites. Their time-orientation is the here and now. They have a high energy level that is coupled with a high need to achieve. Sensors don't usually relax very well; they seem to expend as much energy "relaxing" as most people spend working.

On projects, Sensors are the driving energy to get things done. Give them the task and then get out of the way. They usually require little supervision once they are started. Sensors provide momentum and a sense of accomplishment to the project team. Sensors do not make the best planners but they can contribute excellent information about the work to be done.

The Sensor's potential weakness is the very thing that makes them so valuable; their energy level. If allowed to get away from them, their energy can roll right over slower, less driven team members. Their need for action can lead them to be short-sighted, poor planners and perceived as being rude.

Chapter 4
Project Planning

4

Project Planning

Introduction

Project planning is the most critical single activity on any project. Without a well-thought-out plan, your project is in trouble before you ever start to work on it.

Several points need to be made at the outset:

- Project planning, at least at the beginning, is a sloppy, chaotic, confusing process.

- Project planning is best done by at least some members of the project team as a group activity. It can be done by a single person, but the process presented here is intended for, and results in a better end product when done by, a group.

- Project planning is a repetitive process — it is done in "layers" and the "layers" are created in successive passes through the plan. In the first several passes, flexibility is the key to success. If you try to finalize your plan from the beginning, you'll find that you have forgotten pieces; others are out of their correct order; details are missing; etc.

- Project management software is just that — project MANAGE-MENT software. It is not designed as project planning software and is not, in most cases, appropriate (or even usable) for the planning activity.

- Project plans are almost never "set in stone." At best, they're set in semi-firm Jell-O®. The chances that some part of the plan will need to be changed as the project progresses are almost 100%.

- The finished project plan is the source of all the management tools necessary to track and control the project.

The Important Thing is the *Process* of Planning

" "

Plans are nothing; planning is everything.

Dwight D. Eisenhower
1890-1969
34th President of the
United States

If you are a "just do it" kind of person, this activity is going to be a strain on you. But, it is impossible to overemphasize how important this activity is. The planning process is intended to discover:

- What needs to be done.

- What the appropriate sequence of activities is.

- When activities should start and be finished.

- Who should be doing what, when.

- Which activities can be done in parallel and which must be completed sequentially.

- Where, when, and by whom decisions need to be made.

- Where problems are likely to occur and what impact they might have on the project.

- What deliverables are being created along the way and what criteria should be used to determine their appropriateness.

- Which tasks need closer scrutiny than others.

- Which tasks need greater planning detail than others.

- How resources are to be utilized throughout the project.

- When and by whom major reviews or approvals are needed.

- When and how the final output of project work will be delivered to the customer.

At the beginning of a project, all of this is essentially unknown. What little may be known is usually not in sufficient detail or depth to be of any significant use in the day-to-day management of the project. Developing answers to all of these questions is the purpose of project planning.

The Post-it® Planning Process

" "

A thousand words are worth a picture.

Anonymous

The most valuable and flexible tool available for project planning is the self-stick note — Post-it Notes® by 3-M Corp. and their Highland™ brand. They provide a quick, flexible, inexpensive planning tool that is perfect for dealing with the sloppy, chaotic, confusing mess that is the project planning process.

For most projects, three sizes of Post-it® Notes are sufficient to capture all the essential information for the plan.

*   3" x 5."

*   3" x 3."

*   1-1/2" x 2."

The only other major requirements are:

*   Marking pens to write down the information.

*   A large piece of paper to stick the Post-it® Notes on (30-inch and 36-inch wide roles of white wrapping or banner paper in approximately 50-foot lengths are available at most office supply and stationary stores).

*   Tape to hold the planning paper in place.

*   A wall to stick it on.

Each of the three sizes has its specific use in this process:

*   The 3" x 5" size is used to record the tasks of the project.

> 3" x 5"
> Task Description

*   The 3" x 3" size has two uses.

    *   Placed on the plan as a square, it is used to record sub-tasks or the outputs or deliverables of major tasks or groups of tasks.

> 3" x 3"
> Sub-Task, Task
> Output or
> Deliverable

- Placed on the plan as a diamond, it indicates a decision or approval point. The diamond shape is used to illustrate that there are three possible outcomes to every decision:

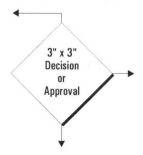

- Approval to proceed (the process arrow goes from the right hand point to the next task).

- Approval denied (the process arrow goes out the bottom point indicating "Stop").

- Approval granted contingent upon some aspect of the work being re-done and re-submitted for approval (the process arrow goes out the top point and loops back to the task that must be re-done).

- The 1-1/2" x 2" size is used to record additional information such as individuals working on a particular task, schedule information, or notes.

The following shows what a developing plan looks like using this technique.

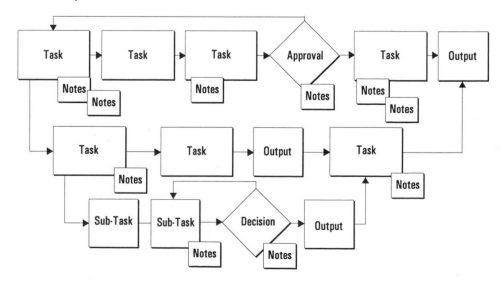

How to Use the Process

As a preliminary, before asking the team to start planning the project, it is a good idea to provide some sort of framework. If you try to begin the process with a large piece of blank paper, most people will have trouble getting started. They need something to start from.

Provide a Framework

The simplest framework is very large pieces of the project placed on the planning sheet as a starting point. These are usually the major phases of the project. For most projects, these phases are very easy to define. In a lot of ways, they are sub-projects. For example, a product development project might have phases like:

- Research.

- Design.

- Prototype.

- Test market.

- Prepare for production.

- Implement production.

A process development project might have phases like:

- Research.

- Design.

- Test and refine.

- Implement.

A software development project might have phases like:

- Specify.

- Design.

- Prototype.

- Code.

- Integrate, test and debug.

- Install and debug (again).

Providing these large building blocks gives the team a context in which to think about the tasks that need to be done to complete the project. Record these phases on the 3" x 5" Post-it® Notes and space them along the top of the planning sheet.

Start at the Highest Level

Have the team brainstorm tasks that need to be done for each phase. Try for the larger pieces of the project first. It is also helpful to ask people to try to think in terms of verb/noun phrases. Combining an action verb with a noun describes both the work that needs to be done and the output of that work better than the noun alone. For example:

• Prepare survey.

• Conduct survey.

• Write functional specifications.

• Build prototype.

• Input data.

• Regression test software.

At this time, it is also a good idea to identify any major decision points you can. Remember, a decision is recorded on the 3" x 3" Post-it® Note posted as a diamond.

As tasks are suggested, write them on the large (3" x 5") Post-it® Notes and stick them under the appropriate phase. At this stage, don't worry about the order of the tasks. This is the first pass at the plan and you should be more concerned with capturing the larger scale tasks under all the phases.

Organize What You Have

When the group seems to be running down, stop for a while and try to organize the tasks. This is the first pass at imposing order on the project. Don't be overly rigid. Simply try to put the tasks in a logical order under each phase. Work horizontally across the planning sheet for tasks that follow one another and vertically for tasks that can be done in parallel. Leave spaces between tasks for additions and details. While doing this, it is likely that other tasks will be suggested as the holes in the plan become more obvious. Write them on Post-it® Notes and stick them in the appropriate places on the plan.

Fine-tune It

When you and the team are satisfied that you have most of the larger tasks in place, ask the following questions:

• What do we have to do first?

• Once we've done that, what can we, or what should we do next?

• Now that we've done that, what can we, or what should we do next?

That third question should be repeated over and over through the entire plan. This activity is likely to spawn even more tasks that we missed in the first couple of passes. Record them and put them where they go.

Add Detail The next stage of this process is to identify those tasks that need further detail in order to be manageable. This is a judgment call on your part. What you need from the plan is sufficient detail so that you can effectively manage the tasks of the project. To do this, you need to know what questions to ask. If you are comfortable that you understand the work involved in a task at this higher level, don't go into detail about it. If, on the other hand, you aren't comfortable with your understanding of the work involved, ask for and record additional details on the task. This will yield a plan in which some tasks are only identified at the highest level while others have two, three or even four additional layers of detail. This plan is your primary project management tool. Make it as detailed as you need.

Connect People to Tasks When you are satisfied that you have sufficient details on the tasks, it's time to start connecting people to them. As much as possible, do this on a volunteer basis. The people in the planning session should be most, if not all of the people who will be working on the project. They are the ones who will be doing the tasks. Ask them to volunteer for those that are appropriate.

You are looking for two levels of involvement in this pass through the plan:

- The person who will be responsible for seeing to it that the task is completed (the person you will ask about progress on the task).

- Anyone who must provide work for the task to be completed.

In many cases, the person responsible will be the person who also does all the work. Therefore, you will have tasks with only one name connected to them. In other cases, particularly at the higher levels of the project, one person will be designated as responsible for a large task that will be sub-divided and worked on by several other people. You need to be able to identify all of them, even though your primary contact about the task will be through the person responsible.

Record people's names on the small (1-1/2" x 2") Post-it® Notes and stick them to the larger task Notes. For tasks with more than one person working on them, indicate the person responsible by writing an "R" on the note with their name. This will make it much easier to locate the responsible people.

Special Note: Have one, and only one, "R" for any single task. For sub-divided tasks, each sub-task should have an individual designated as responsible. If a task looks like it requires more than one person to be responsible, sub-divide the task.

Review the Work Load

Once you've gotten people assigned to the various tasks, take a careful look at the plan. If you see the same name over and over, you may have a problem with over-allocation of one person's time. Look for "underloads" as well as overloads. Do you have someone who is only working on one or two tasks? Can they take over or assist with others? What skills do they have that might be useful on some other part of the project. (Refer to the Skills and Influence Matrix you did during the Pre-Work.)

Get Time Estimates

The next stage of planning is developing estimates of how long tasks will take to complete. Once again, go to the people who will be doing the work. Ask them for their best guess about two types of time estimates:

* Task time. This is the actual work time required to complete the task. How many hours (days) of actual hands-on work are involved in doing the work?

* Duration. This is the time it will take to get the Task time to do the work. Given all the other things an individual has to do, how long will it be from the time the task is started until the finished work can be delivered?

Record these estimates on the small (1-1/2" x 2") Post-it® Notes and stick them to the appropriate tasks. A helpful notation is to indicate Task time with a "T" and Duration with a "D." Durations are your scheduling estimates.

There is a reason for wanting both of these estimates. Let's assume you need to shorten the overall time required for your project. For some reason, this first run at scheduling shows that the project will still be going on seven weeks after the project deadline. (It happens.) If you have two tasks that have the same Task time, say 4 hours, but that have very different Durations, say the first task has a Duration of 8 hours and the second has a Duration of 40 hours, which task has the most room to gain significant time? Obviously, the second task has much more "slack" time. For some reason, it's going to require a full week to complete this 4 hour task. The likelihood of being able to pull several hours, or even several days, out of that Duration is pretty good. It may require some negotiation with the team member and his or her manager, but the impact on the overall timeline of the project is probably worth it.

You need to know both Task time and Duration in order to make good decisions about where time can be salvaged.

In this first run at the project schedule, avoid trying to fit the project into the deadline. Strive for realistic estimates from the team about how long it is really going to take. Remind people to take their existing and potential work loads into consideration when they are giving you their estimates. You will end up with a much better idea of what is involved with your project if you do this.

Find the Critical Path   There is a concept in project planning that is very important for the next round in the planning cycle. It is the idea of the Critical Path that runs through every project.

- The Critical Path is the longest (in terms of time) series of tasks and activities that must be done in sequence.

In every project, there is a straight line series of tasks that have to be done one after the other. In most cases, this is because work on each successive task is dependent on the output of the work on the previous task.

By this time, your plan should have several lines of tasks running through it — tasks that can be done in parallel. You need to determine which of these parallel lines will require the greatest amount of time to complete. This is your Critical Path. Tasks in parallel lines that require less time are not on the Critical Path. These tasks can be completed late (as long as their completion time doesn't exceed the time on the Critical Path) and have no appreciable effect on the overall time required for the project. A delay on the Critical Path delays the delivery at the end of the project.

You can identify the Critical Path tasks by numbering them in sequence on the task-description Notes or in some other way distinguishing them from the non-critical tasks.

Add Up the Critical Path Times   To find out how long your project will take after this first pass at the schedule, simply add together the Durations of all the tasks along the Critical Path. This will tell you how much time you need to remove from the Critical Path in order to come in under the deadline. And, in most projects, you will have to remove time.

Now you can start looking for those tasks with large discrepancies between Task time and Duration. Take them one at a time and see what adjustments can be made.

Re-add the Durations along the Critical Path and see if the project fits the deadline. No? Big surprise.

Now the task of adjusting the schedule becomes somewhat more difficult. There are several things you can look for:

- Additional time from discrepancies between Task time and Duration.

- Adjustments in the order in which tasks are completed. Try rearranging the project in a different order. See if rearranging them will yield a shorter timeline.

- Look for tasks along the Critical Path that don't really have to be there. Look for tasks that can actually be done in parallel with the Critical Path.

- Look for ways to overlap tasks. Is it possible to begin a task with only partial output from the preceding task?

- Look for tasks that could be completed faster with additional resources. Just keep in mind that more people aren't always the answer.

Finalize this Version of the Plan When the group is satisfied that the plan that has been developed through this process represents a realistic view of the work to be done, the people who will do it, and the time it will take to get it done, adjourn the session and prepare the plan for review and approval.

Work on a large surface. A roll of banner or butcher paper makes an excellent working sheet. Tape a long piece (10 to 15 feet) on a wall. Begin by identifying the major phases of the project along the top.

Brainstorm major tasks and decisions within each phase. Don't try to arrange them in order until several have been identified. Use the 3″ x 5″ Post-it® Notes for major tasks. Use the 3″ x 5″ Post-it® Notes, placed as a diamond, for decisions and approvals.

Arrange tasks that must be completed in sequence horizontally across the sheet. Arrange tasks that can be done in paralled vertically in the appropriate relationships with each other.

Add sub-tasks and significant deliverables. Use the 3" x 5" Post-it® Notes for both subtasks and deliverables.

Once all the tasks have been captured, add the names of the individuals who will be involved with each task, sub-task, and decision. Refer to the section on the Responsibility Matrix in this chapter for an explanation of the CAIRO code for identifying each individual's level of involvement in a task. Use the 1-1/2" Post-it® Notes for names.

Next, add the schedule estimates for each task. Remember to include estimates for both Task Time and Duration. Use the 1-1/2" Post-it® Notes for this.

When you are satisfied with the plan layout, add the connecting lines showing the flow of work and the interconnections between tasks. Also include any decision or approval loops.

A built-in loop (such as code, test, debug in software) that may be repeated several times before the work is completed should be enclosed in a dotted-line box. A schedule note should indicate how many times you expect to repeat the process and the duration of the total activity.

Some Additional Planning Tools

The following are additional tools that can be used to document the plan that has been developed. Not all of them are necessary for every project but most will be useful at some time.

Work Breakdown Structure

Work Breakdown Structure is a task list for the project in outline form. Most of the project management software packages on the market require a WBS outline as one of the primary inputs for the program.

Constructing a Work Breakdown Structure outline is simply a matter of taking the tasks captured in the planning process and organizing them as a written outline. Major tasks form the first level of the outline. Sub-tasks form the subsequent levels.

There are two basic outline formats that can be used. The traditional Roman/Arabic alpha-numeric:

I.   A. 1. a. i, etc.

A Work Breakdown Structure using the Roman/Arabic alpha/numeric method would look something like this:

I.   Building Plans Completed
II. Build Offices
    A. Frame walls
    B. Install plumbing
        1. Plumbing rough-work
        2. Finish connections
        3. Install fixtures
    C. Install drywall
    D. Install systems
        1. Install heating and cooling system
            a. Install controls and outlets
            b. Install connections
        2. Install heating and cooling ventilation system
        3. Install fire-suppression sprinkler system
        4. Install electrical and communication lines
        5. Install phones
        6. Install computers
            a. Complete network connections
            b. Test network and systems
    E. Paint walls
    F. Install ceiling
        1. Install gridwork
        2. Install ceiling tiles
    G. Lay carpet and tile
    H. Install moldings and complete finish-work
    I. Clean-up
    J. Furniture delivered
        1. Set up desk and chair groupings
        2. Set up file cabinet groupings
        3. Set up remaining furnishings
    K. Final clean-up
    L. Office construction complete, final acceptance

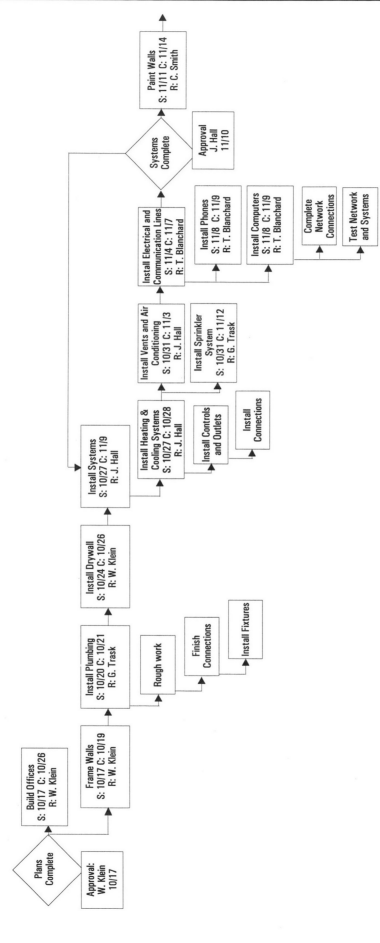

Office Relocation Construction Project
Project Manager: Walter Klein
Prime Contractor: Miller Construction Co.

Enhanced Flowchart:

In this version of a flowchart, the standard information has been enhanced by the addition of the starting (S:) and completion (C:) dates and the names of those responsible (R:) for each task. This combines some of the information from the schedule and the Responsibility Matrix with the graphic display of a flowchart.

In this example, there is an assumption that the sub-tasks fall under the responsibility of the person identified as responsible for the large tasks of which they are a part. Also, there is an assumption that the work of the sub-tasks must be completed within the time frame of the larger task. If this were not the case, schedule and responsibility information could be added to the sub-tasks.

Office Relocation Construction Project
Project Manager: Walter Klein
Prime Contractor: Miller Construction Co.

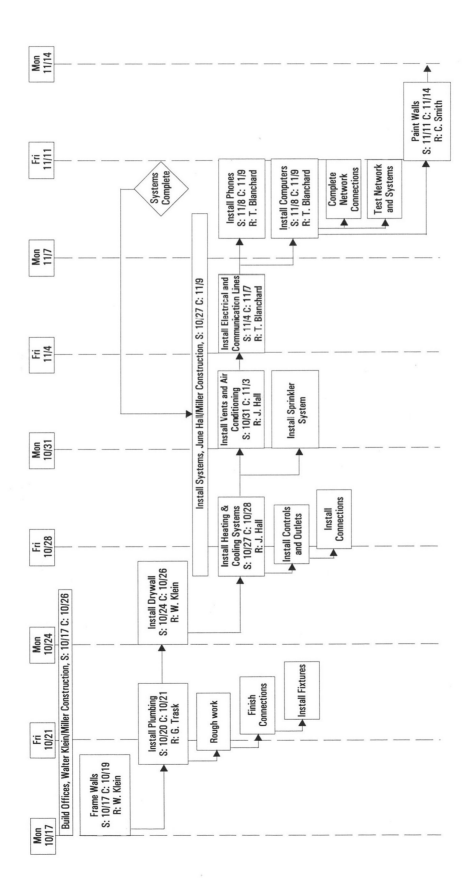

Flowchart Over a Time Grid:

It is possible to lay a flowchart over a time grid and thereby create a combined flowchart and schedule. Usually, the left side of each task box is placed to correspond to the scheduled starting date for that task. Decisions are frequently displayed above the tasks they impact. Summary tasks, such as the "Build Offices" and "Install Systems" groups of tasks, are shown as bars corresponding to the duration of the complete set of tasks that make them up.

Office Relocation Construction Project
Project Manager: Walter Klein
Prime Contractor: Miller Construction Co.

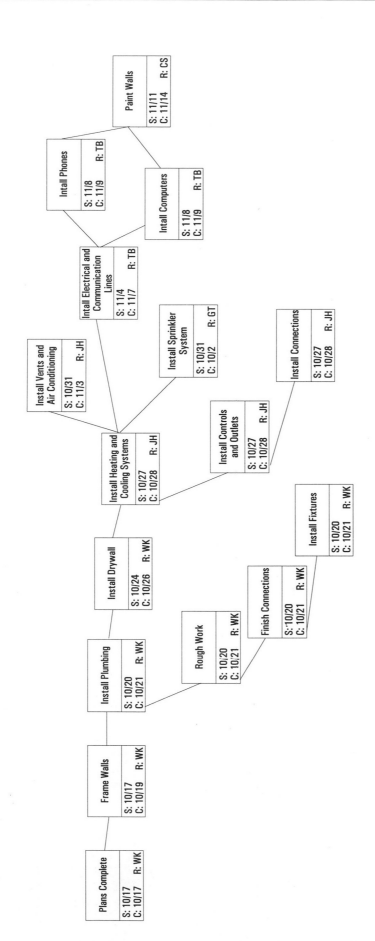

PERT (Program Evaluation and Review Technique) Chart:

A PERT chart is essentially a network diagram showing the relationships between tasks. As of this writing, most automated PERT-charting programs will not allow you to indicate any reverse directional flow of work (such as would occur in a decision or rework loop). Most PERT programs do, however, require the inclusion of starting and completion dates and many also provide for assignment of tasks to individuals.

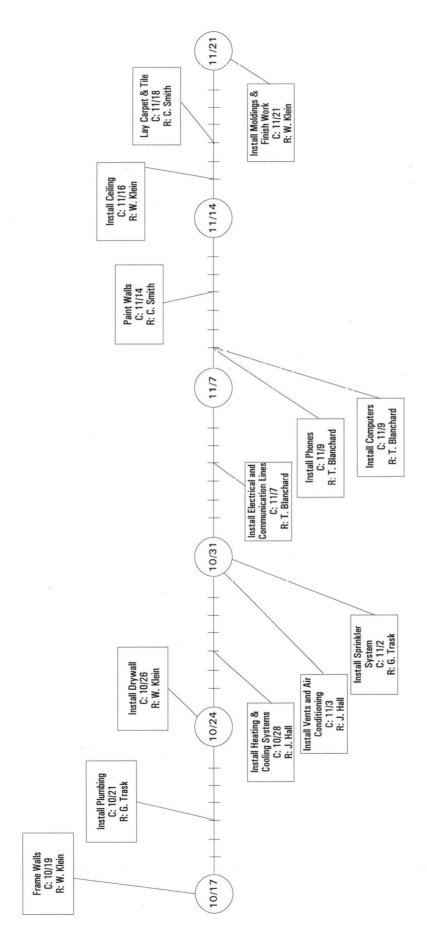

Office Relocation Construction Project
Project Manager: Walter Klein
Prime Contractor: Miller Construction Co.

Timeline Chart:

This chart style uses a central timeline as the base. A convenient time interval is used as a reference (in this case, the dates are all Mondays in the project) and appropriate time intervals are placed between the reference points (in this case, days). Tasks are shown in the boxes. The boxes are connected to the timeline at the starting date of each task. Completion dates and responsibilities are listed in the boxes.

This chart style can be very helpful for building a very quick schedule for a project. However, it does not lend itself to very complex or long-duration projects.

Responsibility Matrix

" "

Leadership appears to be the art of getting others to want to do something you are convinced should be done.

Vance Packard
Journalist

The Responsibility Matrix is an excellent tool for graphically displaying the relationships between the people working on, or stakeholders in, the project and the tasks to be completed.

This tool can be expanded to include not only the project team members but also important stakeholders in the project such as managers and customers. The use of an involvement code can further refine this tool and expand its application to include managing information. Tasks are listed down the left side of the matrix and individuals involved in, or stakeholders in the project are listed across the top. At the intersection of a person and a task, the person's type of involvement in that task is indicated by one of the letters from the word "HART." (For anyone who's interested, Hart is an old English word for the male of the red deer. I know, it has nothing to do with project management but the acronym works.)

- H Helper. This person is contributing work output to the task. This person must schedule time to work on the task and will produce a work product as a result.

- A Ask. This person has information about the task and should be consulted. They do not, however, need to schedule time to work on the task or to produce work output.

- R Responsible. This person is responsible for seeing to it that the task is completed successfully and on time. This is the person you will contact for information about progress. There should be one, and only one, "R" for any task. If it looks like you need to have two or more people responsible for the task, sub-divide the task.

- T Tell. This person should be told about the task. This is the information-sharing code. It can indicate that the person responsible for the next task in sequence should be told that the preceding task is complete. It can indicate that management or some other stakeholder should be updated on progress when a specific task is completed. It can indicate a point in the project where a major project review is scheduled and who will be involved in that review.

Responsibility Matrix

Office Relocation Construction

Project:

Walter Klein

Project Manager:

Janet Hartley, Division G.M.

Project Sponsor:

Team Members and Stakeholders

Tasks	Task Start	Task End	Walter Klein, Project Manager	John Miller, Foreman, Miller Construction	George Trask, Facilities Engineer	Bob Rogers, Foreman, Professional Plumbing	Paul Peters, Foreman, Thomas Drywall	June Hall, Facilities Engineer	Dick Johnson, Foreman, Ace Heating & Cooling	Karl Williams, Foreman, Simpson Sprinklers	Tom Blanchard, Systems Manager	Bill Carlson, Foreman, Acme Electric	Carol Smith, Administrative Assistant	Mary Shiers, Midland Interiors	Steve Andrews, Foreman, Midland Interiors	Harold Bradley, President	Janet Hartley, Division General Manager
Plans complete		10/17	R	A	T		T				T		T			T	T
Build offices	10/17	10/26	R		T		T				T		T				
- Frame walls	10/17	10/19	R	H	T	T	A										
- Install plumbing	10/20	10/21	T			R	H	T	A								
- Install drywall	10/24	10/26	R				H	T									
- Install systems	10/27	11/9	T		T			R	T		T		T				
- - Install heating & cooling sys.	10/27	10/28	T					R	H		A						
- - Install vents and air cond.	10/31	11/3	H		T			R	H								
- - Install sprinkler system	10/31	11/2	H			R	A	T		H	T		T				
- - Install elec. and comm. lines	11/4	11/7	H					T			R	H	A				
- - Install phones	11/8	11/9	T					T			R	H	A				
- - Install computers	11/8	11/9	T					T			R		A				A
- - Systems complete		11/9	T		T			R			T		T	T		T	T
Paint walls	11/11	11/14	T	T										R	H		
Install drop-down ceiling	11/15	11/16	R	H	H	A							T	T	T		
Lay carpet and tile	11/17	11/18	T	T									R	H	H		
Install moldings & finish-work	11/21	11/21	R	H									T				
Clean-up	11/22	11/22	R	H									T	T			
Furniture delivered	11/22	11/22	T											R	H		
Final clean-up	11/23	11/23	T											R			
Office construction complete		11/23	R		T		T				T		T			T	T

Gantt Charts

66 99

The 90/90 Rule of Project Schedules: The first 90% of the task takes 90% of the time available, and the last 10% takes the other 90% of the time.

Arthur Block
Writer and Humorist

The most common format for displaying schedule information is the Gantt Chart. This is a simple horizontal bar chart with the tasks listed down the left and the project timeline across the top. This is a common output of most project management software programs. There are also smaller computer programs that produce only Gantt Charts.

In the example on the following page, additional columns have been added to show responsibilities and task durations. Bars are drawn from the scheduled start to the scheduled completion of each task.

As work is completed, the bars showing scheduled task durations are filled in to show progress. In this example, the following details are illustrated:

- Percent complete.

- Early start.

- Late start.

- Early completion.

- Late completion.

This example also shows Summary Tasks. A summary task is a large group of related tasks. It can be as large as a complete project phase or as small as a single, but complex, task. Most of the software available allows you to display different levels of detail on the schedule. For broad-scope reviews, simply displaying the Summary Tasks is often sufficient. For more in-depth management and tracking, the more detailed levels of task scheduling are important.

Office Relocation Construction Project
Project Manager: Walter Klein
Prime Contractor: Miller Construction Co.

ID	Task	Responsible	Dur.
1	Plans Complete	Walter Klein	0
2	Build Offices	Walter Klein/Miller Construction	8d
3	- Frame walls	Walter Klein/Miller Construction	3d
4	- Install plumbing	George Trask/Professional Plumbing	2d
5	- Install drywall	Walter Klein/Thomas Drywall	3d
6	- Install systems	June Hall/Miller Construction	10d
7	- - Install heat & cool syst.	June Hall/Ace Heating and Cooling	2d
8	- - Install vents and AC	June Hall/Ace Heating and Cooling	4d
9	- - Install sprinkler syst.	George Trask/Simpson Sprinklers	3d
10	- - Install elec./comm. lines	Tom Blanchard/Acme Electric	2d
11	- - Install phones	Tom Blanchard/Wilder Communications	2d
12	- - Install computers	Tom Blanchard	2d
13	- - Systems complete	June Hall	0
14	Paint walls	Carol Smith/Miller Construction	2d
15	Install ceiling	Walter Klein/Miller Construction	2d
16	Lay carpet & tile	Carol Smith/Midland Interiors	2d
17	Install moldings/finish work	Walter Klein/Miller Construction	1d
18	Clean-up	Walter Klein/Miller Construction	4h
19	Furniture delivered	Carol Smith/Midland Interiors	4h
20	Final clean-up	Carol Smith	4h
21	Construction complete	Walter Klein	0

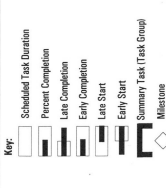

Key:
Scheduled Task Duration
Percent Completion
Late Completion
Early Completion
Late Start
Early Start
Summary Task (Task Group)
Milestone

Gantt Chart:

A standard Gantt Chart lists the tasks down the left and the project timeline along the top. In this example, additional columns have been added to show responsibilities and task durations. Bars are drawn from the scheduled start to the scheduled completion date of each task.

As work is completed, the bars are filled in to show progress: percent completed; early or late start; early or late completion. Milestones (decision or approval points) are indicated by a diamond. The dotted line at Thursday, November 3, indicates the date the chart was updated.

Project Budgets

" "

Under budgetary pressure (arbitrary or not) it is remarkable how many options one discovers one can live without.

J.R. Schlesinger
U.S. Secretary of Defense

Depending on the level of control you have over the financial resources dedicated to your project, you may need to develop a financial budget for your project.

Of all of the items that can be budgeted, labor is the most common. Budgeting labor involves identifying the probable time each team member will need to spend on their portion of the project work and determining the cost of that time. Hourly rates in most organizations include not only the salary of the employee but also a group of expenses sometimes called the "burden." These expenses include the employee's portion of the company benefit package such as health insurance, vacation, and sick time. They may also include a pro-rated overhead expense, or fixed overhead allocation, which amounts to the portion of the overall expenses of operating the business. Your payroll or accounting department is probably the best place to look for these figures.

Once you know how the company accounts for each employee, you can begin to develop a budget that accounts for the labor costs of everyone working on the project. Start by identifying how many hours each team member is expected to devote to the project. It is some times useful to do this in smaller portions, such as individual project phases or significant groups of tasks, rather than for the total project. This is particularly true if the project is to be long (over six months), or if certain team members will only be involved in certain phases or portions of the work.

Budgeting labor expenses is another use for the Task versus Duration breakdown you developed during the scheduling of project tasks. For budgeting, you need to use the Task time as your working numbers. As with most of your project plan, it is a good idea to check with team members to verify your estimates.

Budgeting other items, such as machine time, production capacity, services, etc., follows the same essential process as budgeting labor. Once you know the cost of the item to be used, you can develop a budget to track it.

The Project Budget Checklist in Section 7: **Checklists and Form Masters**, outlines the most common elements of a project budget. Each organization has its own process and format for budgets and the best assistance you can get in developing yours will come from your organization's accounting department. Ask for information and assistance from the people who do this for a living.

The following two forms can be used as worksheets for developing budget information. The first is used to develop labor cost information. The second can be used to develop cost information for other, non-labor budget items.

Special Note: Most of the integrated project management software programs on the market have functions that simplify the development and tracking of these various "budget" items. If you need to track one or more of these, look for a program that has the features you need.

A worksheet for labor budgeting is used to develop the basic information on expected labor usage and expenses. The "rate" for charging labor expenses should be verified with the company's accounting or payroll department prior to developing the budget.

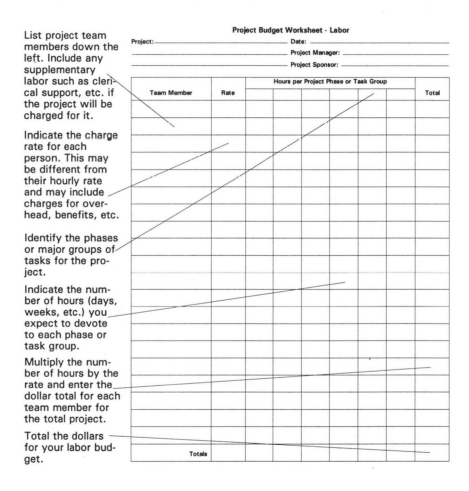

List project team members down the left. Include any supplementary labor such as clerical support, etc. if the project will be charged for it.

Indicate the charge rate for each person. This may be different from their hourly rate and may include charges for overhead, benefits, etc.

Identify the phases or major groups of tasks for the project.

Indicate the number of hours (days, weeks, etc.) you expect to devote to each phase or task group.

Multiply the number of hours by the rate and enter the dollar total for each team member for the total project.

Total the dollars for your labor budget.

List the Items to be budgeted down the side. Include everything for which the project will be charged. This may include such things as raw materials, machine time, and supplies.

Indicate the charge rate for each item and the units by which it is charged (each, dozen, hours, etc.)

List the phases or major groups of tasks of the project.

Indicate how many of each item you expect to use in each phase or group of tasks.

Multiply the number of units by the rate and enter a dollar total for each item for the total project.

Total the dollars for your non-labor budget.

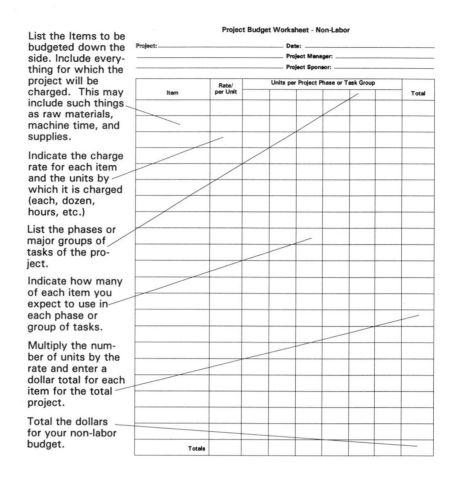

Project Budget Worksheet - Non-Labor

Project: _____ Date: _____
Project Manager: _____
Project Sponsor: _____

Item	Rate/ per Unit	Units per Project Phase or Task Group						Total
Totals								

Contingency Plans

Murphy is alive and well and lurking around waiting to prove that "if something can go wrong, it will." You can't prevent him from messing with your project but you can develop plans for dealing with him when he shows up.

Using the previous work — specifically the work breakdown, project flow chart and project schedule — you should be able to spot a number of points in the project where "something can go wrong." These points are usually connected with critical interfaces between activities: If activity A and activity B are not completed at the same time, a schedule slip is likely; if the vendor doesn't make the delivery schedule, everything will slide; if the solution we think will work, doesn't, we'll have a real problem.

There are certain points in most projects which should always be examined for potential trouble:

- Any point at which two or more activities converge or at which their outputs must be merged.

- Any activity which is effectively out of the direct control of you or the project team. In addition to the obvious things like work being done by outside vendors or other areas of your own company, this also includes decisions and approvals being made by managers not directly involved with the project.

- Any deliverable which, if delayed, will delay the remainder of the project.

Obviously, the first place to look for these points is along the Critical Path of the project. However, don't ignore the secondary and other paths. Sometimes this is where the real problems can occur.

When identifying and evaluating these inside-the-project risks, use the same approach discussed in Chapter 2: **Project Pre-Work**. Evaluate each potential risk for both probability (the likelihood that it will happen) and impact (the consequences if it does happen). Based on this analysis, decide which situations require contingency plans.

Most contingency plans never have to be implemented but, when it does become necessary to use one, it is awfully nice to have it available.

A contingency plan should contain three major components:

- The "trigger event."

- A statement of what to do if the "trigger event" happens.

- A list of who to tell.

The "Trigger Event This is the description of what will tell you that you have a problem. It should be as clear and concise as possible. For example:

- Delivery of raw material delayed.

- Expected outcome not achieved.

- Decision not made on time.

The "trigger event" is your signal to implement the contingency plan. Describe the situation you anticipate and, when and if it occurs, go to plan "B." Don't wait and hope things will get better. They usually won't. They'll usually get worse.

What To Do This is the description of the specific actions to be taken as a result of the "trigger event" occurring. This can be as simple as "contact the alternative vendor," or as complex as a completely re-planned project from this point forward.

Most of the time, the contingency actions fall somewhere in between these two extremes. The important thing is to have a documented plan in place for dealing with the situation. Think of this as a mini-project plan that will be "pasted over" the existing plan in case of an emergency. The level of detail is a judgment call on your part. It should contain sufficient detail to allow you or a team member to track and monitor the work and the effects of that work.

Who To Tell   This is a very important part of the contingency planning process. Every contingency plan should have a list of the people who need to be notified that the project is now on plan "B." Obviously, this list should include the members of the project team. It should also include any managers who have an interest in the project. If the problem is going to affect either the timing or the content of the final deliverable, the customer should also be included.

Contingency Planning Form

Describe the "symptoms: you will see that indicate a problem.

Project: _____   Date: _____
_____   Project Manager: _____
_____   Project Sponsor: _____

Description of "Trigger Event"
_____
_____
_____
_____

Rate both the Probability of the problem occurring and the Impact on the project if it does.

Planning Actions:
_____

Probability: Impact:
☐ High   ☐ High
☐ Medium   ☐ Medium
☐ Low   ☐ Low

Describe any actions that can be taken in the planning of the project to "head off" the problem.

_____
_____
_____

Contingency Plan Actions:

Describe the specific actions to be taken to correct the problem.

_____
_____
_____
_____
_____
_____

Notification List: Notified: Date:

Indicate who should be notified.

Check when each person has been notified and the date of notification.

Major contingency plans should be discussed with the project team during or after the planning activity. This is a "comfort" issue as much as an informational one. It is nice to know that someone has thought about what could go wrong and has made some plans, just in case. This discussion can also result in additional issues that may need to be addressed by contingency plans.

Discussing contingency plans with managers, sponsors and customers is also a good idea. At the very least, you are making them aware of the potential risks faced by the project and you are demonstrating your managerial capabilities by having anticipated and planned for them.

Transfer Plans

" "

Our one major goal is to create satisfied customers. Hence, all systems, objectives, training, and measurements are designed to improve customer satisfaction.

John A. Young
President & CEO
Hewlett-Packard

This is the final piece of the overall project plan package. It is the detail of how you will get rid of the project's output when you're through.

It is important to develop the basic elements of this plan early in the project even though it is likely that some of the details will change as you approach the actual transfer of project output.

This plan should be developed in close cooperation with the project's customer. It should outline, in appropriate detail:

- The various pieces of the final package of project output to be transferred.

- How the transfer will be coordinated.

- Who will be responsible for what parts of the transfer.

- When the transfer will occur and how disruptions in the customer's work, if any, will be handled.

- Details of any on-going support that might be needed once the output is transferred. This should include any requirements for documentation or training that will be needed. If there are any, their development should be included as part of the project plan, just like any other tasks.

Once the transfer plan is developed, you should monitor the project with an eye on the agreed-upon output. It is very common for the ultimate deliverable to change from the beginning of a project to its final hand-off to the customer. Any significant changes should be communicated to the customer immediately.

Even barring significant changes to the output, it is a good idea to schedule a review of the transfer plan somewhere about the middle of the project and again close to the actual point of transfer. These reviews should be included in the project plan as tasks.

Other Planning Issues

In addition to the more "formal" parts of the project plan package described above, there are some additional issues to consider and to plan. The major difference between these and those already discussed is that these are plans you, as the project manager, can develop on your own. Most of them are mainly for your benefit.

Monitoring Plans

" "

If you can't measure it, you can't manage it.

Anonymous

You've detailed a lot of activity that must be completed in order to complete the project. You should take the time to develop a plan for monitoring the critical activities — those that *must* be completed.

There is a trap in trying to monitor too much of the detail of a project. The result is, more often than not, that some of the major activities are allowed to get off schedule. Focusing too narrowly is at least as dangerous as focusing too broadly.

Most monitoring plans are simply notes to yourself of those things you should be watching. Keep these notes on your personal calendar, in your project notebook or even on your copy of one or more of the plan documents. You should have included reviews of work in progress in your overall project plans but these "formal" reviews are not enough to really monitor all the work being done. Here are some tips about which things to monitor:

•   Watch every activity along the Critical Path.

•   Monitor activities leading to points where contingency plans have been developed or are likely to be implemented.

•   Monitor integration points (points where the outputs from two or more activities come together) carefully.

Talk with team members frequently and handle problems as they arise — don't hope they will go away by themselves. They won't. They will just escalate into full-scale crises.

Remember, you have a team made up of "experts" in the various activities of the project. Use their expertise to help with the monitoring process.

Integration

" "

If at first you don't succeed, use a larger hammer.

Anonymous

At some point, various activities associated with the project must be brought together and made to fit. In most projects, this occurs several times. Knowing where these points are (based on the project flow chart and the project schedule), and what must happen when the deliverables are brought together, is the basis of your integration plan. Any tests required to verify that things are working as expected should be included as part of the integration plan.

Depending on the complexity of the activities at each integration point, your plans can be as simple as notes about what should happen. For more complex integrations, it may be advisable to develop more comprehensive plans. These can include a flow chart and schedule for the activity; a responsibility matrix (if enough people are involved); contingency plans, etc.

Every integration is a potential trouble spot. Therefore, every integration should have a contingency plan in case something goes wrong. If the integration doesn't work as it should, delays are likely; some tasks may need to be re-done; additional resources may be required, etc. Think about the integrations that will be needed for your project and plan them carefully.

Management Reporting

" "

Big Brother is watching you.
George Orwell
1903-1950
English Author

You must periodically report your progress to someone. Most likely this will be to some level of management and other stakeholders in your project.

Setting out a plan for doing this and a schedule which details specific reviews and presentations will make your life much easier. Trying to "just keep everyone up to date" in an informal manner is both dangerous and prone to failure.

This plan may be as simple as a schedule of staff meetings where you will give a short update on the project. It may include a format for written reports and "official" management presentations and a schedule of updates and "walk-throughs" for various managers and departments.

However you decide to maintain communication with the people interested in the progress of your project, detailing the activity in a plan will help you ensure that this critical communication is maintained. Remember to schedule these reviews on the Flow Chart, the Schedule and the Responsibility Matrix as project tasks.

Team Meetings and Status Reports

" "

You people [his subordinates] are telling me what you think I want to know. I want to know what is actually happening.
Creighton Abrams
1914-1974
Commander, American Forces, Vietnam

Formal project team meetings are, unfortunately, rare on most projects in most organizations. This is an inconvenience but it is not, necessarily, a major problem. You will be in fairly constant contact with most of the project team.

If you can hold project team meetings, schedule them regularly if possible. A project team meeting is the time and place at which the various team members can update each other. Try to pick a day and time that can be fairly consistent throughout the project. This makes it easier for people to plan for the meeting.

These meetings provide an opportunity for recognizing successes and for dealing with problems before they become disasters. They are also an excellent tool for developing and maintaining the "sense of team" that is critical for project success.

There are some important things to keep in mind about these meetings:

- They are "project" meetings. The agenda should focus on project-wide issues — things of concern and interest to all team members. No one likes to sit through a meeting at which two or three people debate and solve technical issues of no interest to the team as a whole. Keep the meeting focused on broad project issues and handle the individual or small group problems outside the meeting.

- Always have an agenda for the meeting. Distribute it the day before the meeting if possible. A sample agenda format is included in Section 7: **Checklists and Form Masters**.

- Schedule the meeting for a specific length of time (usually one to two hours) and adjourn it when that time has come, earlier if all the agenda items have been covered.

- Always record minutes and distribute them within 24-hours of the end of the meeting. (This is one of the best uses of E-mail. You can even include other stakeholders in the distribution.) A sample meeting minutes form is included in Section 7: **Checklists and Form Masters**.

- Use the meeting as a forum for "cheerleading" and recognizing the successes of team members of the team as a whole.

- A regular part of each meeting should be a status report from each team member. This is discussed in more detail in Section 5: **Project Implementation**.

Deliverables at This Point

The deliverable at this point is the project plan. Whether it is a formal management presentation of the plan, with all the "bells and whistles" or a simple review with the project team, finalizing the plan is a major milestone on any project.

If a formal management presentation is required, give it careful thought. Consider your audience and what they really need to know in order to understand and support your project. Frequently, management presentations take advantage of the ability of many of the project management software programs to "roll up" tasks and schedules into summary detail. Most managers don't need to know all the details of the work to be done. They need an overview of the project. Be aware of the "need-to-know" level of your audience and prepare a presentation that delivers what they need. Be prepared to go into additional detail if requested.

This management presentation is an opportunity to draw attention to significant issues about the project. You should be sure to include the following in your presentation:

- A walk-through of the complete project plan with emphasis on any of the following that are of concern:

  - Major "unknowns" in the project such as not knowing what the research will show or the direction it will require you to take the project; not having enough information about the new technology at this point to make a decision about using it; not knowing the cost of some portion of the project; etc.

  - Tight schedule points where deadlines are likely to be missed.

  - Resource concerns such as limitations, skill levels, availability, etc.

- An explanation of the reporting mechanisms and the frequency with which you will be keeping others informed of progress on the project.

- Any special concerns you might have regarding the project.

NOTE: If you are concerned that your audience may not understand the complexity of what you are about to undertake, you can use the wall chart, created in your planning, as a visual aid. These "rough" plans can be very impressive. Describing the Post-it® Note Process and demonstrating how the project unfolded in the planning shows thoroughness and also lends credibility to your having considered the project from a variety of angles before settling on a final plan.

Issues by Project Type

Process Projects

- Developing a complete analysis of the potential impacts of the proposed process. It is important that the project leader and the project team clearly understand the full implications and impacts of the proposed process. This information can only be obtained by working directly with the people who will use the process and those who support them.

- Determining the internal and external support needed to develop and implement the proposed process. Internal support personnel should be actively involved in the planning process. Depending on the complexity of the proposed process, there may need to be involvement from outside vendors of services and equipment. If needed, information regarding external vendors should be gathered at this stage.

- Identifying pre-process and post-process impacts and how to deal with them. This is part of the development of an overall understanding of the proposed process. It is usually a good idea to develop a "process map" showing the capabilities and limitations of the various process steps and how they inter-relate.

- Identifying critical points in the development process where user (Alpha) tests might be needed. The more complex the process, the more useful incremental tests become. Alpha tests are designed to demonstrate and verify pieces of the process in order to insure that the project is still "on track" and that the various elements being developed meet customer requirements and expectations.

Product/Service Projects

- Defining the exact specifications of the product/service. When developing a product or service for sale to external customers it is important to establish the parameters early in the development process. This sets the boundaries of the development process and can save significant time and money by eliminating certain options before development begins.

- Defining the specific market niche to be addressed. As global competition increases, niche marketing becomes more and more important. One size no longer fits all. Defining the needs and expectations of a specific niche helps focus development activity.

- Identifying internal and external support needed to develop the product/service. Most product or service development projects require extensive support inside the organization and some support from outside. Identifying support needs early allows planning to include them.

- Identifying potential trouble spots in the organization's systems which could impact customer delivery. The world outside the company is usually far more complex and unpredictable than the world inside. Any number of factors could impact delivery of the product or service. Identifying potential trouble spots allows realistic contingency planning.

- Identifying production requirements and ensuring that they can be met. After the product is developed, it must be manufactured. After a service is developed, it must be delivered. Identifying these needs during planning will build most of the elements of the transfer plan.

- Identifying critical points in the development process where customer (Alpha) tests or input might be needed or desirable. Small-scale, incremental tests are always a good idea. They provide information needed for minor (or major) course corrections. Alpha tests are generally tests of "pieces" of the finished product during which potential customers are asked for their input about the direction of development. Usually these tests are arranged and managed by Marketing but some members of the development team should be included.

- Identifying points in development where customer reactions to the product are needed (Beta or Market Tests). Beta tests are generally tests of final prototypes (all the functions of the product or service are in place) and are used to develop information for final fine-tuning before production begins. Beta tests are also generally arranged and managed by Marketing and should include some members of the development team.

Software Projects
- Defining the exact specifications of the software (functionality, user interface, platform requirements, media for distribution, etc.). As with any project, software projects need clear parameters within which to operate. Given the speed and scope of development in computer software, it is perhaps more important to establish boundaries in this type of project than in most others. Necessary performance is the key — don't add bells and whistles that don't directly affect the application of the software to the problem being addressed.

- Defining the process needs to be addressed for the customer. This is the means by which the limits of performance can be set. What does the customer need the software to do? How will it be used? What other programs will need to integrate with it? Etc.

- Identifying internal and external support needed to develop the software. Support for software development projects usually involves a number of functions other than writing code. There is documentation to be developed, packaging to be designed, reproduction and distribution to be completed, after-sale (or after-installation) support to be established, updates to be scheduled.

Externally, there is retail sales to be developed, distribution channels to be established, demonstrations to be scheduled, etc. You need to know these requirements in order to effectively plan the development and transfer plans.

- Identifying when Alpha (limited functionality) and Beta (full functionality) tests are needed. Alpha and Beta tests are very important in software development projects. Software development seems to deviate from customer needs far more easily than other types of projects and, therefore, the "course-correcting" that can be achieved through incremental testing is more necessary.

- Setting limits on "raw" research. This is an outgrowth of the speed and complexity of computer development. Most new applications require some degree of "pure" research — research which simply looks at what is possible given the current state of the art. However, this research should be focused on finding information that will aid in developing a product that will meet customer needs, not on finding out how much functionality can be crammed into the program.

- Establishing the integrations requirements (with other software, with various operating systems, etc.). This is also part of the process of bounding the development process. What other programs will need to integrate with the developing program? What systems will be supported? Etc.

Chapter 5
Project Implementation

5

Project Implementation

Introduction

The activities of daily project management are essentially cyclic in nature. They follow a pattern of: Monitoring, measuring, problem-solving and reporting.

But first, the project has to get underway.

In this chapter, you will look at:

- Getting the project started — Project Kickoff.

- The cycle of project management including: Monitoring and measuring work output; status reporting; task management; people management; information management; project documentation; change control; and, problem-solving.

- Some tips on keeping things moving once you've gotten them started.

Project Kickoff

Once the planning is completed, it is time to launch the project. This
event should be marked with some sort of ceremony. The larger the
project, the larger the ceremony. The smaller the project, the less
grandiose the event, but there should still be something that marks
the actual beginning of project work.

The opening event of a project should be appropriate for the significance of the project. For a really significant project such as the development of a new product or a radically new piece of software, a fairly
significant opening event is appropriate. This can entail an off-site
meeting at which the project team works through a simulation of the
project, spotting potential trouble spots and developing a sense of team-
work. It can be a formal announcement to the organization that the project is underway, and a "pep talk" about its impact if successful.

Smaller-scale projects can be launched with a simple meeting of the
project team. This can be done over coffee or can be a scheduled
meeting with a full agenda.

The point to having an opening event is to signal the start of the project. This is more for the team than for the organization. This marks the
beginning of some concentrated work for the team and a little recognition of that fact. It is also recommended that there be a closing event
for the project. This is discussed in Section 6: **Project Closure.**

**Content of the
Kickoff**

Regardless of the size of the project or the kickoff event, there are a
couple of things that should be covered:

- A review of the plan and schedule.

- A review of the "ground rules" for the team and the project.

As discussed in Section 2: **Project Pre-work**, and in Section 4: **Project
Planning**, most of the key players on the project should have been involved in the development of the project plan. There are, however,
additional players on most projects. These are the support personnel
who will play limited, but nonetheless critical roles in the project. The
project kickoff is an appropriate point to involve all the players in a review of the project.

**Review of Plans
and Schedule**

This review should include:

- A walk-through of the plan and the schedule.

- A discussion of the major milestones throughout the project.

- A walk-through of the major contingency plans.

Be prepared to answer questions or provide additional information. This is the team's chance to voice concerns and expectations about the project. Allow for this.

Set the Ground Rules In reviewing the "ground rules" you should make your expectations clear. People will generally do what you want them to if they know what it is. Some of the issues you should consider including in this part of the meeting are:

- The need for constant, clear, honest communication about project activity.

- Your expectations about participation in the work of the project as well as in project meetings and reviews.

- How conflicts will be resolved and how problems will be solved.

- How you will keep the team updated on progress and issues of project-wide concern.

- What you expect from team members in the way of status reports, when you expect them and what you will do with the information.

Laying out these expectations up front, and getting agreement about them, will save massive headaches later in the project.

There is another element that can, and usually should, be included in the kickoff: Cheerleading. A little "motivational" talk about the importance of the project to the organization (or some part of it), and a reminder of the importance of success to each team member is always in order. Don't try to turn a simple project into the moon landing project but try to find encouraging and "inspirational" words for whatever projects you work on.

The Cycle of Project Management

Once the project is under way, your job as a project leader is one of monitoring, measuring, problem-solving and reporting. This cycle begins on the first day of the project and continues right up to, and sometimes even after, the handoff at the end.

Monitoring and Measuring

" "

Information gathering is the basis of all other management work, which is why I spend so much of my day doing it.

Andrew S. Grove
CEO, Intel Corp.

The monitoring and measuring activities are constant and totally intertwined. Whatever you monitor, you also measure.

The project leader's job during this phase is truly one of management — of ensuring that what needs to be done gets done, on time, within budget and meeting performance standards.

Due to the lack of true managerial authority being granted to most project leaders within organizations, much of this "management" must be done through the use of influence that is not backed up by hierarchical power. This doesn't make the situation impossible, just more interesting. The project leader's ability to negotiate, convince, compromise, and get people to perform will be tested throughout the rest of the project.

Having a committed team, strong support from the project's sponsor, customer and management, and a good set of project plans are the keys to successfully carrying out your project. If you encounter situations you cannot resolve, ask for help — either from team members or from management or others within the organization (such as Human Resources). Remember, your job is to get the project done, not to do it all yourself.

One specific tip about asking for help: Never present a problem without also offering your ideas about how the problem could be solved. This does two things:

- It shows that you have thought about the situation and are actually asking for confirmation that your solution should be implemented. This will get you a reputation for solving problems rather than simply dumping them on someone else.

- You will find that, more often than not, your proposed solution will be the correct one. This also enhances your reputation as a problem-solver.

Monitoring and measuring (managing) the tasks of the project involves implementing the monitoring plans you've developed. Your plans should allow you to:

- Track activities by individual, by time and by budget (if applicable).

- Spot problems early.

- Make course corrections quickly.

- Gather the information necessary to make valid decisions.

Your job is primarily to coordinate activity — not complete the project yourself. One of the most dangerous traps for inexperienced project leaders lies in trying to "do" too much of the actual work on the project.

An integral part of monitoring and measuring is some form of regular status reporting from team members. If you can hold regular team meetings, this is the forum of these updates. If you can't hold regular team meetings, there are other ways to gather this information.

Status Reports

" "

Information may be accumulated in files, but it must be retrieved to be of use in decision making.

Kenneth J. Arrow
Nobel Laureate
in Economics

You can rely on your ability to contact everyone on the project team on a regular basis — usually once a week — and depend on your memory and some notes to always ask the right questions. This is not recommended.

You can request a regular, written status report from each team member. If you are going to use this approach, provide the team with a format for reporting. A recommended format follows.

Compiling and summarizing the status reports from your team and adding your own status report is an excellent way to create a status report for management.

Project Status Report

Project: _____ Name: _____
_____ Date: _____
_____ Interval Since Last Report: _____

Please complete and submit this form weekly. Give specific details of activities, challenges, actions and plans. Use additional pages if necessary for complete information. Thank you.

Describe activities and accomplishments since the last Status Report was submitted.

Activities/Accomplishments: Since your last Status Report, what have you accomplished on your project work?

Describe any problems encountered or discoveries made while working on tasks.

Challenges/Discoveries: In the course of doing your project work, what problems did you encounter and what discoveries did you make?

Describe any actions taken on problems or discoveries.

Actions Taken on Challenges/Discoveries: What did you do about problems or challenges you encountered: actions taken, results achieved, individuals informed, etc.?

Describe activities planned before the next scheduled Status Report.

Planned Activites: What are you planning to accomplish prior to your next scheduled Status Report?

Task Management

The management of tasks also involves people, information and problem-solving. As the project leader you are the focus of project activity. You are the one who will be asked to "fix it" when things aren't going right. You will be the one asked to make decisions, settle disputes, find resources, answer questions, etc. In order to do all of these things successfully, you must be aware of what is going on, in all aspects of the project, all the time.

There are several specific things you can do that will help you maintain a good overview of project activity:

•   Be accessible. Don't lock yourself away from team members. Get out and walk around. Talk with team members whenever you see them. Hold quick, casual, "how's-it-going" meetings.

•   Ask questions. The normal, reflexive response to, "How's it going?" is, "Fine." Sometimes that's true. But, sometimes it isn't. You should be aware of what each individual or group should be doing and asking specific questions will frequently uncover small problems that have the potential to become large crises.

•   Update the project plan and schedule daily. If it is possible to hold a "stand-up, work-of-the-day" meeting each morning, this is the perfect time to update the posted plan and schedule. If the daily meeting is not possible, wander around the project team early in the day and gather the information needed to update the information. Doing this will not only keep you informed but will also encourage team members to work to have progress to report.

•   Deal with problems immediately. If you uncover a problem (or a potential problem) deal with it. If you can solve the problem on the spot, do it. If the problem requires the participation of others, take, or assign, the responsibility of getting the required people together as soon as possible. If you assign this responsibility to someone else, make arrangements on the spot to be informed of the results of the meeting. Be specific about what information you need.

•   Implement contingency plans as necessary. The chances are very good that you will have to implement one or more of your contingency plans before the project is completed. If this becomes necessary, be sure to inform everyone on the team that the direction has changed. Tell management about the situation and detail what you are doing (and are going to do) about it. Tell your customers about it. Be sure that everyone understands the trade-offs that will result from the change in direction. Change the posted project plan and schedule to reflect the new situation and be sure that individual's plans and schedules are also updated.

•   Never miss an opportunity to recognize success, effort or good work. Saying "good job," "nice work," or "thank you," takes virtually no time. These simple phrases are some of the most powerful in the English language when it comes to encouraging people to perform well.

Managing People
" "

Human beings are compounded of cognition and emotion and do not function well when treated as though they were merely cogs in motion. ... The task of the administrator must be accomplished less by coercion and discipline, and more and more by persuasion. ... Management of the future must look more to leadership and less to authority as the primary means of coordination.

Luther H. Gulick
President and Chairman,
National Institute of
Public Administration

Maintaining the project team as a team; dealing with conflicts and problems between team members and between the team and other functional areas; and, ensuring that individual issues do not prevent progress on the project are also your responsibility.

Project teams generally work well. It seems that the opportunity to do something new and different energizes people and helps create the sense of shared responsibility and cooperation that is the hallmark of a good team.

However, even the best of teams have times when things don't work as well as they could. Team problems must be dealt with as soon as they are discovered or they will begin to affect the output of the team members.

In some organizations, interpersonal issues are not openly addressed. They are suppressed in favor of "professionalism" and "focusing on the task." Emotion is viewed as "unprofessional" and not acknowledged. We may be professionals but we are also people. We have emotions and they can get banged up. Trying to ignore them only makes the problem worse. The more technically-oriented a project team, the greater the tendency to suppress people issues in favor of task issues. This is a very dangerous tendency. People are unique individuals, with individual wants and needs. They are not machines designed to perform tasks. The problems that destroy project teams are rarely technical in nature. They are usually emotionally based. Managing these issues is a significant part of your job. Refer to Section 3: **People Skills for Project Leaders**, for information on some of these issues.

Managing Information
" "

Effective management always means asking the right question.

Robert Heller
Editor

You will succeed or fail based on the quality of information you have, and pass on, about your project. Information is the life-blood of a project. The nature of projects makes them information-intensive.

- You need to know just about everything that is going on all the time. You also need to maintain the "document trail" for the project by keeping pertinent information in a log or file.

- Team members need to know about activities that will affect their tasks, how their work will integrate with the work of others, when things need to be done, where to find necessary information or assistance, how to solve problems, etc.

- Management needs to be kept informed about progress, problems, successes, needs, etc.

- The customers of the project need to be informed about progress, changes in the basic design, timing of incremental tests, issues around the transfer of the project results, etc.

The vast majority of the responsibility for keeping information clean, current and moving, rests with the project leader.

Getting the Information You Need

The best way to get information is to ask for it. Your requests for information should be specific and should include a time-frame within which the information needs to be provided.

Several information-gathering tools should be built into the project plan. But, gathering information on an on-going basis is still necessary for successful project management. Most of your information needs can be met through individual contact with team members. Project meetings or regular status reports from team members will provide most of the other information you will need.

Team Member Information

" "

An individual without information cannot take responsibility; an individual who is given information cannot help but take responsibility.

Jan Carlson
CEO, Scandinavian Airline System (SAS)

Daily contact with members of the project team is an opportunity for information to flow both ways — from them to you and from you to them. These "meetings" need not be formal. On the contrary, they should be quick, to the point and focused on the issues at hand. Most of the time (unless a major problem comes up) these information-passing encounters will take less than five minutes.

When it is either necessary or desirable to get some information in writing, ask that it be kept as brief as possible while still giving all the pertinent details. Keep written information in an organized file that will allow you to find it again if needed.

Management Information

" "

This report, by its very length, defends itself against the risk of being read.

Winston Churchill
1874-1965
British Statesman and Prime Minister

At some time during the life of a project, you will need to make some sort of presentation to management. This may be a simple one-on-one meeting at which you go over the status of project activity. It may be a full-blown "event" with overheads, demonstrations, presentations by team members, etc.

There are some key points to keep in mind when preparing for a management presentation:

- Most managers are not interested in the details. They need to know the information necessary to make decisions. They do not need to know all the "nitty-gritty" details of the project. Keep information to management in summary form. Use a "bullet-point" format for written information. Provide an overview of the issues with only as much detail as is required for a good understanding of the overall situation. If detailed information is needed, provide it in a separate document attached to the summary.

- Never present a problem without a possible solution attached. You have been granted some management authority by being made a project leader. Along with that comes management responsibility.

  A large part of that responsibility centers around problem-solving. You may not be in a position to solve a problem completely. That may be why you are making a management presentation (to ask for additional resources, assistance, etc.). But, you should have some idea of how the problem can be solved. You should be asking for assistance in implementing your proposed solution.

- Present your plans for future activity. Bringing management up to date is only half the job. You also need to let them know what you are going to do next. At the end of a presentation, summarize the steps to be taken next and tell them when you will be updating them again.

Customer Information

" "

Use your own best judgement at all times.
Entire Contents of Nordstrom Corporation Policy Manual

Getting information about project actvity to the project's customers (or their representatives) is also important. If your customers are inside the organization, including them on the routing of meeting minutes or status reports will take care of most of their information needs. Including key internal customers in management presentations is also a good way to keep them informed. Involving internal customers in the periodic tests and evalutations of parts of the project is also an excellent way to keep them informed.

If your customers are outside the organization, their information needs are likely to be much less demanding and can usually be met by the customer representative on the project team. This can be done through market tests, focus groups, alpha and beta tests, etc.

Project Documentation

Different projects require different levels of on-going documentation. Whatever documentation you have decided is necessary for your project should be updated on a regular basis — daily if possible, never less than weekly. Keeping a notebook or log on the project is the simplest way to maintain information. This can be done on paper or on computer. However, if you are keeping information on a computer, also maintain a file for various pieces of information which are not on the system such as hand-written notes, plan drawings, etc.

Change Control

Changes occur on almost every project. Sometimes they are minor and don't have much impact. At other times, they are so major they require re-thinking the entire project, changing the constraints, getting new resources and moving the deadline.

Most project changes fall somewhere between these two extremes. The issue here is to have in place a system to document the changes made to the project. For this purpose, some form of change control documentation is a good idea.

The following form is an example of a Change Control Document that can be used as a model. Using this form, you can document requested changes as part of your on-going project documentation. It can serve as a part of the history of how the project evolved and also as documentation of the decisions and actions taken regarding alterations to the project plan and the project's output.

Project Change Control Document

Project:_____   Requested by: _____
_____   Date: _____
_____   Received by: _____

Describe the requested change in detail. → **Description of Requested Change:**
_____
_____

Rate the priority of the change.

Indicate the impact of the change in terms of time, resources, output.

Priority: **Description of Impact:**
☐ High   _____
☐ Medium   _____
☐ Low   _____

Describe the impact of the change. → **Impact:**
☐ High   _____
☐ Medium
☐ Low

Describe any modification of the request or how long it will be on hold. → ***Length of "Hold" or Description of Modification:**

Decision:
☐ Proceed   _____
☐ Hold*   _____
☐ Modify*
☐ Do Not Change _____

Check the decision about this change.

List individuals who should be told about the change or the decision. → **Notification List:**   **Notified: Date:**
_____   ☐ _____
_____   ☐ _____
Check and date when notified. _____   ☐ _____
_____   ☐ _____
_____   ☐ _____
Get authorization for the change. _____   ☐ _____
_____   ☐ _____
Date the decision and the action.

_____   _____   _____
Date of Decision   Date of Action   Authorizing Signature

Problem-Solving

" "

Don't duck the most difficult problems. That just insures that the hardest part will be left when you're most tired. Get the big one done — it's downhill from then on.

Norman Vincent Peale
Clergyman and Author

First, you don't have to personally solve every problem that comes up. If you try to, you won't get much else done. You have a team of people who are quite capable of solving most of the problems they encounter. Let them.

On those occasions when your personal involvement is needed, most of the time it will be in the form of guidance, facilitation, decision-making or direction-setting. The rest of the time it will be a need for your technical expertise. Whenever possible, guide team members toward finding a solution rather than "fixing it for them."

When someone comes to you with a project-related problem, your first response should be something to the effect of, "What do you think we should do about this?" Encourage team members to always bring possible solutions along with their problems. You will find, over time, that most people who are bringing you a problem are either asking for permission to implement a solution they have already developed or for a decision about which of a list of possible solutions they should try first. Do not fall into the trap of trying to solve every problem personally. You won't be able to do it and people will quickly learn that if they don't want to deal with a problem, all they have to do is give it to you.

In the Appendices of this book there is a problem-solving process model and several problem-solving tools which can be very helpful in dealing with the major problems that can surface during a project. The caution about using this process is that it is very data-intensive and time-consuming. It should be reserved for problems that do not have readily apparent solutions.

Keeping It All Moving Ahead

" "

It's kind of like herding cats or pushing on a rope.

Anonymous

The activities of daily project management are continuous and cyclic. You will go through the routine of monitoring, measuring, problem-solving and reporting, over and over. It is this constant contact with the project and the project team that keeps you informed and on track.

There is a concept that applies to most projects as they are implemented. It is the idea of "momentum." Most project activity starts out rather slow and sporadic. As the project begins to develop, the pace picks up. The energy level of the participants increases and the work gets done faster. As the project nears completion, the level of activity in almost every area will intensify. Last-minute decisions will have to be made about functions and capabilities. Integration problems will have to be solved. Plans for the transfer of project results will have to be finalized.

You can learn to utilize the "momentum" that builds in your projects to focus activity and keep things on track. Unfortunately, this is not a skill that can be easily taught. The best you can do is to watch your projects and identify those times when the pace seems to "ratchet up" a notch. Look for the reasons for the increased activity. Look for ways to intentionally increase the pace at critical points in the project. Over time, you will get a sense of when and how to "nudge" project activity along.

You should do all of the following activities to some degree throughout your projects. As the project nears completion, however, most of them will become more intense. These are things you can do to keep things under control:

- Be available. Spend time with the team.

- Be calm. Even if you're feeling stressed, try not to let it affect how you interact with others. They will be looking to you to set an example.

- Be prepared to make tough decisions. Chances are you will be called upon to make one or more decisions about what to include and what to leave out of the final package. You need to be ready to make these decisions and to be ready to justify your decisions to management and to your customers.

- Be positive and encouraging. Your team will be looking to you for reassurance that "this is all going to work out alright." Being positive and encouraging does not mean you ignore the problems or gloss over their significance. It does mean that you help the team maintain a "can do" attitude.

- Communicate, communicate, communicate. Communicate with everyone who needs to be informed about how things are going. Keep information flowing in every direction.

- Keep the relationships you need to get the work done in good condition. Thank people for their assistance. Recognize both successes and good trys that didn't work. Offer assistance but don't take over someone else's tasks.

- Document what you do. The best way to learn from an experience is to be able to go back over it and look at what went right and what went wrong. Keep a simple log of activities related to the project. The things you most want to capture are notes about:

  - What worked.

  - What didn't work.

  - How problems were discovered.

  - How problems were solved.

  - Key discoveries made in the course of the project.

Issues by Project Type

There are some special concerns that surface depending on the type of project being undertaken. These are issues the project leader should watch carefully during this period.

Process Projects

• Obtaining commitment from all parties to support the project. This issue centers around the need for realistic commitments of time, personnel and other resources needed to complete the project. Pay particular attention to the need for higher levels of support as the project nears transfer.

• Development team orientation. Be sure to stress that the final output of the project must smoothly integrate with existing operations and that these operations are to be actively involved in the development process.

• Development team reporting relationships. Clarify who reports to whom about what. It is more likely that individuals will be faced with the "split-loyalty" issue on this type of project than on others. Clarifying these relationships early will avoid problems later.

• On-going verification of activities with customers. Since your customers are inside the organization, this should be an easy process. It is particularly important to maintain close communication with your customers regarding any changes to the original plan, schedule or specifications of the project.

• System impacts further defined. As the project progresses, the interaction of the proposed process on other processes should be reexamined and the impacts redefined if necessary.

• System changes made incrementally. In almost every process change, it is possible to "evolve" the new process in stages which can be carefully monitored and adjusted as needed.

• High level of interaction with the ultimate recipient. The final customer should be involved closely in the activities and decisions throughout the project. Since the customer is internal, this should not present significant problems.

• Frequent, small-scale tests of the pieces of the final process. Most processes are composed of several operations working in sequence or in parallel. Testing the process incrementally as each step is developed can prevent delays and misdirected development.

• Constant monitoring of changes in peripheral processes. This is particularly important if the project is part of a larger program of improvement or change. If supporting or dependent processes are being altered concurrently, it is very important to monitor changes in those processes to determine their impact on the project.

Product/Service Projects

- Obtaining commitment from all parties to support the project (can include key customers, key distributors, etc.). Product or service development projects tend to impact a significant portion of an organization (particularly as they near transfer). They also have impacts outside the organization that need to be considered. If, for example, market tests are to be conducted, now is the time for marketing and some members of the project team to begin to develop the plans for implementing those tests.

- Development team orientation (should include marketing representation). The project team should be clearly grounded in the *customer need* that is to be addressed by the project. The involvement of marketing in the project should be clearly defined.

- Development team reporting relationships. Clarify who reports to whom about what. Stress the need for constant focus on the customer need being addressed and the processes which will support that focus.

- On-going verification of project activities with customers. In most cases, this interaction will be with a representative of the customer group. It is important that there be some direct contact with potential buyers of the product or service during the project.

- Prototype (Alpha) tests completed. As the product is developed to the point where a customer can be asked if the overall direction of development is correct (functionality present but not necessarily in final form), an Alpha test should be conducted.

- Production (Beta) test completed. As the product nears final form (functionality complete and most of the features operational), a Beta test should be conducted. This will frequently take the form of a small market test.

- User documentation completed and verified. Packaging, labels, instructions, etc., need to be prepared and any legal requirements met.

- Production systems prepared. The operations that will produce the product must be tested and capabilities verified.

- Distribution systems prepared. The means of getting the product or service into the hands of the consumer must be tested and capabilities verified.

- Customer support systems prepared. The methods of supporting the consumer in the use of the product or service, warranty and service systems, etc., must be readied and verified.

- Market introduction plans finalized. Announcements, press releases, advertising, "grand openings," etc., must be planned and readied.

- Customer feedback system prepared. The means of gathering information and determining acceptance of the product or service must be implemented.

Software Projects
- Obtaining commitment from all parties to support the project (can include key customers/users, platform suppliers, etc.). Software development projects usually require a high level of coordination between the software developers and support functions such as documentation development. Commitments and agreements need to be obtained from all interacting parties about their individual requirements.

- Development team orientation (should include either a key user or a marketing representative with a clear understanding of the user's process needs). Once again, the need for focus on the process needs of the ultimate user should be strongly reinforced as should the limitations around the functionality to be included.

- On-going verification of activities with customers. User needs are frequent and must be continuously redefined and tested against the direction of development.

- Prototype (Alpha) tests completed. Most software is built as separate functions which operate under a common controlling system. It is usually possible to test individual, or small groups of related functions before the complete program is assembled. This can help insure that the necessary features are being developed and included. These tests are usually conducted at the developer's site.

- Regression testing and debugging. As various pieces of the final package are completed they should be integrated and tested for interaction (regression tests). Debugging the software should be done carefully and a new test of the integration should be run after each bug is corrected to insure that no new problems have been introduced.

- Production (Beta) tests completed. Once the final integration has been completed and all regression tests have been run, Beta tests of the program in a typical user's environment should be conducted to verify that functionality and features meet user needs.

- User documentation completed and verified. Since the instructions for installing and using the program will likely be developed in parallel with the software, final documentation should be verified against the final functionality and features of the software.

- Production system prepared. The means of transferring the software from the development system to the user system (disk, magnetic tape, CD-ROM, etc.) should be readied and tested for accuracy.

Chapter 6
Project Closure

6

Project Closure

Introduction

Once the project plan has been executed, project activities completed (as far as the plan is concerned), and the project deliverables made ready for transfer to operations, it is time to gain the approvals needed to actually transfer the project results to the customer.

This process is another negotiation stage in the life of the project. Negotiations at this stage are between the project leader (and possibly the core team) and:

- The project's sponsor.

- The project's customer.

- Any support groups who will be asked to maintain the results of the project in the customer's environment.

If the transfer plan (created as part of the project plan package) has been updated regularly, if the customer has been involved (either in person or through a representative), if management has been informed of project activity, and if the support groups have been involved as necessary, this process is simply a matter of formalizing the agreement that the project is ready to transfer.

However, that is a lot of "ifs." The chances are fairly good that one or more of these groups needs to be brought up to date on the project before it is actually transferred. There are four major issues which should be considered during this process:

- Documentation and/or training needed.

- Timing of the transfer.

- Implementation process.

- On-going support.

The decisions on all of these issues should be documented in the final version of the transfer plan.

Documentation and Training

" "

Through training your employees
you can have a greater degree of
confidence that the work will progress through a pattern that you
designed.

William F. Cone
Manager of Professional
Development, Hughes Aircraft

Some documentation of project output is needed for virtually every project. This can be as simple as a written description of the characteristics of the project output — what does it do? It can be as complex as an operating manual containing detailed instructions about how to use the project output.

Whatever the documentation needed, it should be written in *the customer's language and terms*. Keep in mind the people who will be using the project output and document it in terms they can understand and can use.

The output of many projects requires some degree of training to be carried out during the implementation process in order to fully meet the customer's needs. This training should be fully developed as a part of the project deliverables. Training can be conducted by project-team members (as in the case of internal process projects and some software projects) or it can involve training by others (as in the case of product or service projects requiring outside-customer training by customer support personnel). Even these projects usually require participation by members of the project team in training the trainers.

As with project documentation, training materials can be simple or complex. They should also be written in customer terms and should provide sufficient information for the customer to effectively use the project results.

Negotiations around these issues should focus on whether the documentation and training meet the needs of the customer and management. Adjustments may be necessary.

Timing of the Transfer and Implementation Process

" "

Once someone understands you respect his time, he will be more
willing to speak with you.

James Dennis
Director of Marketing
Communications
Hewlett-Packard

Particularly on initial process and software projects, this is the big one during this stage. Exactly when and how are you and the project team going to implement the project output in the customer's environ-ment? What involvement will customer personnel have in the imple-mentation? What support will be needed from other groups? How long will the implementation take?

The majority of this negotiation will be between the project leader (and possibly core-team or other project-team members) and the cus-tomer. Virtually every project, regardless of the type, requires a close working relationship between the project team and an internal cus-tomer. Some of the elements of this issue are:

*   When should transfer start?

*   When should transfer be completed?

*   Who will perform which tasks?

*   What are the disruptions that are likely to occur in the customer's work patterns during transfer?

*   How will the disruptions be managed?

*   What are the contingency plans needed to cover possible prob-lems?

*   How should the training and implementation be coordinated?

*   How will final adjustments be performed and by whom?

*   What "fall-back" options exist if the implementation must be aborted?

*   What are the indicators that the transfer is complete?

Answering these questions before the actual transfer begins generally results in a smoother process and the least disruption to the cus-tomer's work patterns.

On-Going Support

Few projects end with a total hand-off — absolutely no more involve-ment by project team members. Some level of on-going support is usually needed for a period of time after the project is made opera-tional in the customer's environment. In some cases, this is simply a need to have someone available to answer questions as they arise. In other cases, it involves assigning project-team members to the cus-tomer to provide support over an extended period.

This issue should be carefully examined and the transfer plan should be updated to reflect these needs. The appropriate assignments need to be made and, if the requirements are significantly different from those originally anticipated, the affected project-team members and their managers should be involved in the negotiations.

Completing the Transfer

" "

Even if you're on the right track, you'll get run over if you just sit there.

Will Rogers
American Actor and Humorist

This encompasses all the activities which must be completed in order to make the project output fully operational in the customer's environment. The actual timing of fully meeting this milestone will vary greatly depending on the level of on-going support required from the project team by the customer. This milestone is fully met only after the project team has ceased to have any responsibilities for the implementation of project output. The transfer is not complete until the customer no longer requires assistance from project-team members to use the output of the project.

If long-term support is anticipated, arrangements should be made to assign project-team members to the customer, as a work assignment separate from the project. This will allow the project to be closed and still provide the assistance required.

This is the period when you "tie up the loose ends" of the project in preparation for closure. Some kind of "acceptance of project output" should be executed when the output is implemented. This provides a specific point in time when the project is finished.

Projects have a tendency to "take on a life of their own" and to just keep going long after the project plan activities have been completed. This is one of the most common problems with ending a project on time. The transfer plan (which should be agreed upon by all affected parties) should contain specific, measurable criteria for determining when each piece of the project has been transferred. Once all of the pieces have been transferred, the project is over. Gathering all of the loose ends can drag on for a very long time if these criteria are not established and used.

A final transfer document can be prepared which states the criteria for completed transfer and which also outlines those things which are the customer's responsibility (such as ensuring that individuals needing training are available for training, that on-going maintenance has been arranged, that on-going operational needs are understood, etc.). This document need not be complex but it should be complete and should clearly state the criteria for completion of the project.

Closing Out the Project

Pack it in. Put it away. Bid it goodbye. Every project comes to an end. That is one of the main things that separates projects from on-going business activities.

This period of time is focused on closing out all aspects of the project and documenting the lessons learned. Some of the things that should be completed during this stage include:

- Closing out all work orders, purchase orders and other accounting paperwork.

- Preparing project documentation (your project log and supporting materials) for archiving.

- Disbanding the project-team.

- Preparing the final project report.

- Holding the "post mortem" for the project.

- Holding the "closing ceremonies" for the project.

Accounting Closeout   There will likely have been several pieces of paperwork generated during the project that require a final close-out to complete the paperwork cycle. These should be finished as part of the project-closure process.

Archiving Project Documentation   The various documents and materials which make up the record of project activities need to be organized and filed so they can be retrieved as needed. There are both practical and legal reasons for doing this.

From the practical side, other project teams may be able to use materials, formats, information, etc., developed during your project to help them with planning or implementing theirs. At the very least, project documentation forms a part of the on-going records of the business.

From the legal side, project documentation provides legally valid records for such things as patent and trademark applications, defense in lawsuits, defense of proprietary information and processes, etc.

Some organizations have a central archive of some sort where this information can be stored. If no central archive is available, keep a file yourself.

Disbanding the Project Team

The extent to which personnel were devoted to the project will determine how complex or time-consuming this process will be. On very large projects, the project leader has a very real responsibility to see that project-team members are successfully reintegrated into their work assignments. Discussions with each member's functional manager are a good idea. These discussions should cover certain points:

- A report on the person's participation on the project team.

- A discussion of the skills and knowledge the person gained from the project experience.

- An evaluation of the person's performance on the project.

- A sincere "thank you" for their support and contribution of the team member's time and expertise to the project. Even on smaller projects, remember that "thank-you-note-evaluation" option.

Final Project Report

Once again, the complexity of the project determines the complexity of this report. Simple projects may only require a one-page summary of what happened. More complex projects may require a significant documentation effort including details of research discoveries, future lines of research, significant successes and problems, etc. This report should be completed as close to the end of the project as possible.

Post-Project Evaluation

This is an important activity in which all of the project team and others who can provide valid input (such as customers, vendors, etc.) should participate. The more successful the project was, the more fun this process will be. But, the more problems encountered and the more difficult the project, the more important this process is.

You are trying to determine several things through the post-project evaluation:

- What went right? Why?

- What went wrong? Why?

- What contingency plans had to be implemented? Why?

- What totally unexpected events impacted the project?

- How well did the project plan package guide the project?

- How well did the project team, as a whole, perform?

- How well did the information systems which supported the project work?

- How did you do as a project leader?

- What advice would the project team give to someone about to undertake a similar project?

The post-project evaluation should be held as closely as possible to the actual end of the project so that information and experiences do not have a chance to become "clouded by the passage of time." There are a couple of cautions that go along with this:

If the project was a great success and everything went well with the team, you can hold this evaluation meeting as soon after project closure as possible.

- If, on the other hand, the project was less than a resounding success, if there were some problems with the team, if there are some outstanding issues among team members, you may want to hold off on this meeting for a week or so. This gives people a chance to "put some distance" between themselves and the experience.

Under no circumstances should you wait more than two weeks after the end of the project to hold this evaluation meeting. Any longer and the information you get may not be that useful.

Closing Ceremonies

Some sort of "event" (no matter how small) should be planned for the official end of the project. Again, the size and complexity of the project dictates the extent of this event. But, even if it is only a short meeting of the project team at which you express your appreciation for the efforts of all members, a closing event adds the final touch to a project. It brings things to an end in everyone's mind and provides a final opportunity for team members to interact in the context of the project.

Issues by Project Type

Process Projects

- Obtain agreement from all parties about the timing and methodology for implementing the new process. Process implementations almost always result in disruptions in the customer's work patterns. These disruptions should be minimized as much as possible and the customer's on-going production needs should be considered.

- Verify training and/or documentation needs. Process implementations usually involves far more people than could practically have been included in the actual project. The means of transferring the information they need to use the project results is a critical consideration.

- Define short-term and long-term support plans. There will almost always be an overlap between the end of the project and the final activities of project-team members in the customer's environment. Sometimes this involvement can extend over several months. Clear definition of the needs, resource requirements and customer expectations about this support is important.

- The customer takes delivery of the results of project activity. The new process is made operational in the customer's environment. Operators are trained, machinery (if needed) is installed, operational tests are conducted, adjustments in supporting processes are made, the process begins operation.

- Implementation assistance is provided. The various members of the project team with expertise in the new process provide assistance to the customer in making the process operational. The focus is on getting the customer's personnel fully acquainted with the process and how it works.

- The customer performs acceptance tests and provides feedback for adjustments (if needed). As the process is implemented, the customer evaluates the operation and provides information to the project team about acceptability. If adjustments are needed to fully meet the customer's needs, they are made, keeping in mind that trade-offs are still an issue and that significant changes will require approvals.

- The customer evaluates the total project. This is the customer's input to the final review of the project that will take place upon completion of the transfer. The customer should be asked to provide feedback on the total project including such issues as the level of cooperation during development, the extent to which expectations and needs were met, the quality of the final results, the process of implementation, etc.

- On-going support (if needed) is established. Short-term support to be provided by project-team members (as part of the project) should be scheduled. Long-term support (that which is not part of the project plan) should be arranged and any documentation or training needed to ensure quality should be provided.

- Project documentation is carefully organized to serve as a guide for future, similar projects. The documentation of process projects should be organized in such a way that future project leaders dealing with similar projects can use the processes and experiences of your project as a guide and a source of information about what to anticipate. It should also include full explanations of any proprietary developments.

- Implementation impacts are studied for possible enhancements. The issues which surfaced during the transfer and implementation of project results should be studied for clues to other improvements that could be made. Any significant discoveries should be carefully documented and brought to the attention of individuals who are in a position to make decisions about their importance.

- Critical learnings/discoveries are documented for future projects. Clues about how to "work the system" within the organization should be provided for future projects.

Product/Service Projects

- Final adjustments in production/delivery systems are made. The "fine-tuning" of the production and delivery systems that will produce and deliver the product or deliver the service should take place at this time. Contingency plans should be developed to solve any potential problems.

- Pre-introduction samples are prepared and delivered. In most product/service projects, there is a short period of time during which sample products or service demonstrations are delivered to selected representatives of the customer group. This can involve press releases, product or service demonstrations at trade shows, full-scale geographically-specific market introductions, etc. This activity also allows for further fine-tuning of production and delivery systems.

- Distribution/delivery systems are verified. Few organizations maintain direct control over the entire process of delivery into the hands of the ultimate customer. The capabilities of vendors of distribution and delivery services need to be verified and any adjustments made.

- Production begins. The first actual production runs of the product or customer delivery of the service are started. The production process is monitored for a specified period of time to ensure that all is working well.

- Distribution begins. The delivery of product to customers is started. The delivery system is monitored for a specified period of time to ensure that all is working well.

- The customer support system is implemented. This usually involves completing training of customer support personnel. Criteria for completion should be developed.

- Initial customer feedback is evaluated. The initial market reaction to the product or service provides information for the final evaluation of the project. It can also provide information for future product or service enhancements or clues to additional needs which can be met.

- Project documentation is carefully organized to serve as a guide for future, similar projects. An important part of this process is the documentation of proprietary discoveries made during the project. Also, significant "short cuts" or work practices that proved useful should be documented.

- "Next generation" products/services are defined. The chances are great that everything that could be included was not included in the product or service, most likely due to time constraints. Those elements which "had to be left out" should be documented for the next project dealing with the product or service.

- Critical learnings/discoveries are documented for future projects. Clues about how to "work the system" within the organization, directions for future products and services, and any other significant information about possible future projects should be documented.

Software Projects

- Final integrated system tests completed. The program should be tested in every conceivable configuration in which it might be used by the customer. Any bugs detected should be addressed either through an adjustment to the program or by an addendum to the user documentation clearly detailing the limitations or conditions under which the bug is likely to surface and how the user can work around the problem.

- Production systems are tested. This usually involves actually producing copies of the program using the production system and comparing the code, line for line, against the original.

- Production begins. There are two aspects to this depending on whether the software is for internal use or for external sale. For internal use, "production" means the customer begins using the software to perform work. For external sale, "production" means software duplication.

- Initial customer feedback is evaluated. From internal customers, this feedback includes comments on ease of use, accuracy, speed, etc. From external customers, it includes market survey responses. The purpose of this feedback is to define refinements, improve ments and the direction of future development projects.

- Project documentation is carefully organized to serve as a guide for future, similar projects. An important part of this process is the documentation of proprietary discoveries made during the project. Also, significant "short cuts" or work practices that proved useful should be documented. Bits and pieces of code not used should be stored for possible use in enhancements.

- "Next generation" or enhanced products are defined. Most software goes through several revisions and enhancements during its functional life. Many of the elements of these enhancements are a direct result of work done on the original project which couldn't be included in the first release due to time constraints. This work should be documented.

- Critical learnings/discoveries are documented for future projects. Clues about how to "work the system" within the organization, directions for future products, work methods developed, short cuts in the programming or testing process, etc., should be documented for future projects.

Chapter 7
Project Planning and Management
Checklists and Forms

Project Planning and Management Checklists

Needs Analysis Phase Checklist

☐ A project leader has been selected.

☐ The project's Customer has been identified.

☐ The problem to be addressed by the project has been defined.

    ☐ Needs have been identified and verified.

    ☐ Wants have been identified and weighted.

    ☐ Alternative solutions have been developed.

    ☐ Alternatives have been compared to Needs and those not meeting all identified needs have been eliminated.

    ☐ Alternatives have been screened through the Wants.

    ☐ Risks have been evaluated.

    ☐ The best alternative has been selected.

☐ The constraints have been identified:

    ☐ Time (starting date, due date, any significant milestone dates).

    ☐ Resources (people, materials, money).

    ☐ Output (performance or quality characteristics).

☐ A project Sponsor has been identified and has agreed to support the project.

☐ Stakeholders in the project have been identified.

☐ The core members of the project team have been identified.

☐ The first draft of the project goal has been completed.

    ☐ Connection of project goal to organizational goals has been established.

☐ Preliminary planning has been completed.

☐ Planning resources have been requested.

☐ Project goal has been approved.

☐ Priority of the project has been established.

Project Planning Checklist

☐ Planning has been done with the key players involved.

    ☐ Project has been flow-charted including:

        ☐ Phases of work.

        ☐ Major tasks in each phase.

        ☐ Major deliverables in each phase.

        ☐ Key decisions/approvals.

        ☐ Sub-tasks and detail tasks.

        ☐ Responsibilities and involvement.

        ☐ Schedule estimates.

☐ Responsibility Matrix has been completed.

    ☐ Commitment gained from all managers contributing to the project.

    ☐ Commitment gained from all team members for the work they must complete.

☐ Relationships and interdependencies between tasks identified and confirmed.

☐ Task assignments negotiated with each team member and agreement gained about:

    ☐ The deliverable to be provided.

    ☐ The estimated <u>task</u> time required.

    ☐ The estimated <u>duration</u> of the task.

    ☐ The assistance or resources required to complete the task.

    ☐ The responsibility and authority to complete the task.

☐ The project schedule is complete:

    ☐ Conflicts have been resolved and known "trade-offs" have been negotiated.

    ☐ The critical path has been established.

☐ Contingency plans have been developed for:

    ☐ Each major or critical milestone (specifically those along the critical path).

    ☐ All "high impact" risk conditions throughout the project.

☐ Costs have been developed for all external resources (non-staff personnel, materials, etc.) and a budget has been prepared.

☐ Project goal has been completed and includes time and resource factors.

☐ Customer's priority and project priority have been reconciled.

☐ Additional plan details (project leader's monitoring and other plans) have been completed.

☐ Project Plan approved by appropriate management.

If the scope or any other significant project parameter changes, negotiate the changes and repeat the Project Planning Phase and the Needs Analysis Phase if necessary.

Project Implementation Checklist

☐ Hold an appropriate project "Kickoff" event.
On a regular basis, remember to:

☐ Manage project priorities, considering time, resources and performance parameters.

☐ Hold regularly scheduled project-team meetings or collect status reports from all team members.

☐ Replan based on progress-to-date, changes in priorities or changes in any of the "triple constraint" parameters.

    ☐ Always evaluate changes in resources, time and performance parameters for impact on the project before committing to them.

☐ Track and document all changes to the project.

☐ Keep everyone associated with the project updated with frequent status reports.

☐ Manage Customer Expectations. Be sure your customer is expecting what you will deliver.

☐ Implement contingency plans if needed:

    ☐ Inform the customer of the change.

    ☐ Involve the team in the decision.

    ☐ Inform everyone associated with the project of the change.

☐ Talk to team members daily.

☐ Facilitate work.

☐ Remove obstacles.

☐ Refine and update the plan to transfer project results:

    ☐ Work closely with the customer.

    ☐ Involve anyone who may be impacted by implementation of the project.

    ☐ Define who will do what, when.

    ☐ Define how disruptions in the customer's work patterns will be managed.

    ☐ Refine the completion criteria.

Project Transfer Checklist

☐ Transfer plans have been reviewed and finalized with the project's customer.

☐ Project results meet the completion criteria in the transfer plan.

☐ All training and documentation has been prepared and is ready to present to the customer.

☐ The customer has accepted project results.

☐ Follow-up, enhancement or extension projects have been identified.

Project Closure Checklist

☐ Organizational documentation related to the project (accounting, work orders, etc.) has been completed and submitted.

☐ The Post-project evaluation has been completed.

    ☐ It included all of the project team, the customer and others who had valid input.

    ☐ Results of the Post-project evaluation have been documented.

☐ On-going support for the customer (if appropriate) has been established.

☐ Final project report has been written and submitted.

☐ Project documentation has been archived.

Project Goal Checklist

The project goal should be tested and verified through a series of dialogues with both the management that is responsible for the project and the customers of the project. Is the project goal:

Yes No

☐ ☐ Specific enough that there can be no doubt about the desired final outcome of the project?

☐ ☐ Measurable in terms that are appropriate for determining when the goal has been achieved and whether the project has answered the need which caused its creation?

☐ ☐ Agreed upon by everyone who will be affected by the project? This will include management, customers, support and maintenance functions.

☐ ☐ Realistic in the sense that the project falls within the expertise of those who will work on it, that it is appropriate for the business and in terms of the resources available for its completion?

☐ ☐ Time-framed as realistically as possible to meet the real needs of the customer and the business?

Project Objectives Checklist

Objectives should be developed for every major activity of the project. Objectives should be function-specific and developed under the same criteria as the project goal. Are the objectives:

Yes No

☐ ☐ Specific? Define the exact nature of the deliverables expected and tie them to the accomplishment of the project goal.

☐ ☐ Measurable in terms that are appropriate for the function and the tasks to be performed? This should also tie into the measures that will be applied to the total project.

☐ ☐ Agreed upon by the functional manager and the project participants from that function?

☐ ☐ Realistic in terms of the abilities and expertise of the function and the resources available.?

☐ ☐ Time-framed to meet the overall needs of the project schedule and the needs of other functions with which the group or individual must interact?

Plan Assumptions Checklist

Plan assumptions should be developed and shared with everyone who is affected by the project. Assumptions should cover those things over which project personnel have little or no direct control but which could seriously impact the project. Each assumption should be tested and verified if possible. Have you asked the following questions:

Yes No

☐ ☐ What factors inside the company do we assume will support project activities?

☐ ☐ What factors inside the company do we assume will restrict project activities?

☐ ☐ What factors outside the company do we assume will support project activities?

☐ ☐ What factors outside the company do we assume will restrict project activities?

☐ ☐ How should we rank these factors in their order of importance to the project?

☐ ☐ How can we test each assumption?

☐ ☐ Have we tested each assumption?

Work Breakdown Checklist

Developing the work breakdown for the project should begin at the highest level of activity and proceed, step by step, to the lowest appropriate level of detail. This process begins at the level of group or individual objectives. For each objective, ask "how will this be accomplished" between three and five times. Have you:

Yes No

☐ ☐ Determined the objectives for each individual or group involved with the project?

☐ ☐ Determined how the highest level of activity for each objective will be accomplished?

☐ ☐ Determined how each successive level of activity for each objective will be accomplished (as far as you believe it is necessary for you to understand and assist).

☐ ☐ Determined your level of involvement in the accomplishment of either the objective or some activity leading to its accomplishment?

☐ ☐ Verified the work breakdown with the people who will be responsible for accomplishing the objectives?

Project Flow Chart Checklist

The flow chart developed as part of the planning activity is the basis for all subsequent project planning. It is a graphic representation of the series of activities and deliverables that will lead to the accomplishment of the project goal. Remember to identify the Critical Path through the project:

- The **Critical Path** of the project is the longest single string of events and activities along the project. If a delay occurs in an activity along the critical path, the whole project is delayed.

It is sometimes helpful (depending on the complexity or duration of the project) to construct several flow charts based on manageable pieces of the project and to then combine these into a single flow chart for the total project. Ask the following questions in the process of gathering information for the flow chart:

Yes No

☐ ☐ Do you know the significant deliverables throughout the project?

☐ ☐ Do you know what activities must be completed in order to accomplish each deliverable?

☐ ☐ Do you know what peripheral activities support major activities?

☐ ☐ Do you know the order in which activities must be completed?

☐ ☐ Do you know which activities result in critical deliverables (those which must be completed before succeeding activities can begin)?

☐ ☐ Do you know who is responsible for each activity?

☐ ☐ Do you know the time estimate for each activity?

Project Schedule Checklist

The project schedule is best displayed as a Gantt chart which lists tasks or activities down the vertical axis and time along the horizontal axis. Before constructing this chart, do you know:

Yes No

☐ ☐ The critical activities of the project?

☐ ☐ The order in which they must be accomplished?

☐ ☐ The Task-time estimates for each activity?

☐ ☐ The Duration-time estimates for each activity?

☐ ☐ Which activities connect at critical deliverables?

An alternative to the "task/duration" method of collecting time estimates requires that you ask for three estimates for the duration of a task:

- The Optimistic time (if all goes well, how long will it take to deliver?).
- The Pesimistic time (if everything goes wrong, how long will it take to deliver?).
- The Most Likely time (in your best judgement, what is a realistic estimate of how long it will take to deliver?).

The following formula can be used to calculate time estimates when there is a significant discrepancy between any of the estimates for optimistic, most likely and pessimistic time required to complete a task:

$$te = \frac{ot + 4mlt + pt}{6}$$

te = time estimate
ot = optimistic time (the time required to complete the activity under ideal conditions)
mlt = most likely time (the most realistic time estimate under normal conditions)
pt = pessimistic time (the time required to complete the activity under the worst conditions.

To develop the time estimate, add the optimistic time to four times the most likely time and the pessimistic time. Divide the result by 6.

Does your method of updating the project schedule allow you to show progress on an activity in terms of:

Yes No

☐ ☐ The activity is on schedule?

☐ ☐ The activity is ahead of schedule?

☐ ☐ The activity is behind schedule?

☐ ☐ The activity is completed?

Responsibility Matrix Checklist

There should be no event or activity on either the project flow chart or the project schedule which does not have a specific individual responsible for its accomplishment. Events and activities are listed down the vertical axis and individuals are listed across the horizontal axis. The intersection of an event or activity and an individual should show that person's level of involvement in the accomplishment of the task.

The CAIRO code is useful for indicating levels of involvement:

C = Consult — this person has information which is necessary to complete the task, but they do not need to schedule time to work on it.

A = Advise — this person should be told about the task; specifically when it is started or completed. (Also used to indicate when to inform management and customers about progress.)

I   = Involved — this person must be involved in the work of completing the task; they must schedule time to work on the task and produce work output.

R = Responsible — this person is responsible for seeing to it that the task is completed.

O = nO involvement — this person is not involved in this task. (A "no involvement" intersection on the matrix can simply be left blank.)

The responsibility matrix should be discussed with each individual shown on the matrix and their agreement to accept the various responsibilities assigned to them should be obtained. Have you:

Yes No

☐ ☐ Specified one, and only one, individual responsible for every task?

☐ ☐ Discussed involvement with every person listed on the chart and received their commitment?

☐ ☐ Verified that all activities have been included?

Project Budget Checklist

Budgets should be developed in cooperation with the functional areas involved in the project and with the assistance of accounting personnel if possible. Does your budget include:

Yes No

☐ ☐ Estimated direct labor costs?

☐ ☐ Estimated indirect (support) labor costs?

☐ ☐ Overhead and fringe benefits? (Most companies have a formula for this computation; check with accounting.)

☐ ☐ Estimated materials costs?

☐ ☐ All other anticipated expenses related to the project?

The budgeting process can also be applied to non-monetary things such as time available, equipment usage and availability, etc. Just remember to "budget" in the appropriate "currency", i.e., hours, machine through-put capacity, etc.

Contingency Plan Checklist

A contingency plan should be developed for each significant event along the critical path of the project. Plans should also be developed for points where significant risk has been identified. Does each contingency plan include:

Yes No

☐ ☐ The event or events which will signal the need to implement the plan (the "trigger" events)?

☐ ☐ The specific actions to be taken to implement the plan?

☐ ☐ The specific changes implementation of the contingency plan will cause in the total project plan?

☐ ☐ A means of analyzing the total project plan for unexpected impacts?

☐ ☐ A list of individuals who should be notified that the contingency plan has been implemented?

Monitoring Plan Checklist

The monitoring plan is your tool for anticipating and dealing with the problems which will occur during the project. Does your monitoring plan allow you to track:

Yes No

☐ ☐ Differences between planned start dates and actual start dates for each activity?

☐ ☐ Differences between planned finish dates and actual finish dates for each activity?

☐ ☐ The percentage of completion for each activity and for the project as a whole?

☐ ☐ Activities performed out of sequence?

☐ ☐ Milestones achieved or missed?

☐ ☐ Differences between estimated costs and actual costs for activities and the project as a whole?

☐ ☐ Differences between estimated resource requirements and actual resource requirements for activities and the project as a whole?

☐ ☐ Activities, issues or individuals of particular importance or concern?

Integration Checklist

The integration plan is the tool for ensuring that critical interdependencies and interconnections between activities are considered and carried out. Does your integration plan allow you to determine:

Yes No

☐ ☐ Which activities result in deliverables which must be integrated with deliverables from other activities and how they must integrate?

☐ ☐ Which points in the project are appropriate for testing the results of interconnected activities?

☐ ☐ What criteria should be used to determine the success of the integration?

☐ ☐ What specific elements of the performance or quality criteria can be tested at each integration point?

☐ ☐ Who needs to be involved in the integration, testing and the evaluation of results?

Management Reporting Checklist

The management reporting plan is your plan for keeping various managers and other interested parties informed about project activity. Does your management reporting plan include:

Yes No

☐ ☐ Who needs to be kept up to date on the project?

☐ ☐ Their level of "need to know"?

☐ ☐ How they can best be informed based on their level of "need-to-know"?

☐ ☐ An appropriate schedule of updates?

☐ ☐ The points during the project it is likely (or certain) that formal management presentations will be needed?

☐ ☐ A general format for management presentations?

Team Meeting Checklist

The team meeting schedule should specify the basic information team members will need in order to prepare for and schedule participation in meetings. Does your team meeting schedule and plan include:

Yes No

☐ ☐ The frequency, duration and location of regular project-team meetings?

☐ ☐ The general agenda format for meetings?

☐ ☐ The format for minutes which will be taken and distributed?

☐ ☐ A distribution list for meeting minutes?

Status Report Checklist

Status Reports should be collected from all team members on a weekly basis. Do your Status Reports include:

☐ ☐ The tasks accomplished since the last status report?

☐ ☐ The problems or discoveries encountered while working on the project?

☐ ☐ The actions taken, or the people informed, about the problems or discoveries?

☐ ☐ The plans for future activity?

Transfer Plan Checklist

The initial transfer plan, developed as part of the project plan package, will likely be updated several times as the project progresses. The basic concerns of the transfer should, however, be outlined and whatever detail is available should be included. Does your transfer plan include:

Yes No

☐ ☐ The specific deliverables to be handed over at the end of the project and to whom they are to be delivered?

☐ ☐ The documentation and training which will accompany the transfer of deliverables?

☐ ☐ The timing of the transfer?

☐ ☐ The process of the transfer?

☐ ☐ The customer's involvement in the transfer?

☐ ☐ How disruptions to the customer's work will be overcome (if appropriate)?

☐ ☐ The test and measurement criteria by which the customer will judge the acceptability of the deliverables and the implementation?

☐ ☐ The anticipated level of on-going support that will be needed, how long it will be needed and who will provide it?

Post-Project Evaluation Checklist

Everyone who can provide you with valid input (team members and others) should participate in this post-project review. Have you asked the following questions:

Yes No

☐ ☐ What went right? Why?

☐ ☐ What went wrong? Why?

☐ ☐ What contingency plans had to be implemented? Why?

☐ ☐ What totally unexpected events impacted the project? (Why were they unexpected? Could they have been anticipated? How could they be anticipated on future projects?)

☐ ☐ How well did the project plan package guide the project? (How could it have been better?)

☐ ☐ How well did the project team, as a whole, perform? (What could have made it better?)

☐ ☐ How well did the information systems which supported the project (internally and outside the project itself) work? (What could have made them better?)

☐ ☐ How did you do as a project leader?

☐ ☐ What advice would the project team give to someone about to undertake a similar project?

Project Planning and Management Forms

Alternative Rating Form

		Alternatives					
Wants	**Weight**						
	Total Points						

Instructions:

List the Wants to be evaluated in the first column. List their Weight in the second column. List the Alternatives to be compared across the top. Work across, evaluating each Alternative against each Want, one at a time. Assign a score to each Alternative that reflects how well it satisfies the Want. Multiply the score by the Weight for that Want. Enter the total in the Alternative column. Total each Alternative column.

Commitment Analysis Form

Project: _____ Date: _____

_____ Project Manager: _____

_____ Project Sponsor: _____

Individual	Commitment Needed	For	Against	Unsure

Skills and Influence Matrix

Team Members

Project:

Project Manager:

Project Sponsor:

Skills Needed

Individuals to be Influenced

Responsibility Matrix

Team Members and Stakeholders

Project:

Project Manager:

Project Sponsor:

Tasks	Task Start	Task End													

Project Budget Worksheet - Labor

Project: _____ Date: _____

_____ Project Manager: _____

_____ Project Sponsor: _____

Team Member	Rate	Hours per Project Phase or Task Group						Total
Totals								

Project Budget Worksheet — Non-Labor

Project:_____   Date:_____

_____   Project Manager:_____

_____   Project Sponsor:_____

Item	Rate/ per Unit	Units per Project Phase or Task Group						Total
Totals								

Contingency Planning Form

Project: _____ Date: _____

_____ Project Manager: _____

_____ Project Sponsor: _____

Description of "Trigger Event":

_____

_____

_____

_____

_____

_____

_____

Priority: **Impact:**   **Planning Actions:**

☐ High   ☐ High   _____

☐ Medium   ☐ Medium   _____

☐ Low   ☐ Low   _____

_____

_____

_____

_____

Contingency Plan Actions:

_____

_____

_____

_____

_____

_____

Notification List: **Notified: Date:**

  ☐

_____ ☐ _____

_____ ☐ _____

_____ ☐ _____

_____ ☐ _____

_____ ☐ _____

_____ ☐ _____

_____ ☐ _____

Project Status Report

Project: _____   **Name:** _____

_____   **Date:** _____

_____   **Interval Since Last Report:** _____

Please complete and submit this form weekly. Give specific details of activities, challenges, actions and plans. Use additional pages if necessary for complete information. Thank you.

Activities/Accomplishments: Since your last Status Report, what have you accomplished on your project work?

_____

_____

_____

_____

_____

_____

Challenges/Discoveries: In the course of doing your project work, what problems did you encounter and what discoveries did you make?

_____

_____

_____

_____

_____

_____

Actions Taken on Challenges/Discoveries: What did you do about problems or challenges you encountered: actions taken, results achieved, individuals informed, etc.?

_____

_____

_____

_____

_____

Planned Activites: What are you planning to accomplish prior to your next scheduled Status Report?

_____

_____

_____

_____

_____

Project Change Control Document

Project: _____   **Requested by:** _____

_____   **Date:** _____

_____   **Received by:** _____

Description of Requested Change:

_____

_____

_____

_____

_____

_____

_____

Priority: **Description of Impact:**

☐ **High**   _____

☐ **Medium**   _____

☐ **Low**   _____

Impact: _____

☐ **High**   _____

☐ **Medium**   _____

☐ **Low**   _____

*Length of "Hold" or Description of Modification:

_____

Decision: _____

☐ **Proceed**   _____

☐ **Hold***   _____

☐ **Modify***   _____

☐ **Do Not**   _____
    Change

Notification List: **Notified: Date:**

                                                                          ☐
_____   ☐ _____

_____   ☐ _____

_____   ☐ _____

_____   ☐ _____

_____   ☐ _____

_____   ☐ _____

_____   ☐ _____

_____   _____   _____
Date of Decision   **Date of Action**   **Authorizing Signature**

Meeting Agenda

Meeting Time: _____ **Duration:** _____ **Location:** _____

Meeting Purpose: _____

_____

Expected Outcome: _____

_____

_____

Participants:

_____   _____

_____   _____

_____   _____

_____   _____

_____   _____

Topic:	**Person Responsible:**	**Time:**

Review action items and assignments.

Develop agenda for next meeting.

Critique this meeting.

Meeting Minutes

Meeting Time: _____ Duration: _____ Location: _____

Meeting Purpose: _____

_____

Expected Outcome: _____

_____

_____

Participants:

☐ _____   ☐ _____

☐ _____   ☐ _____

☐ _____   ☐ _____

☐ _____   ☐ _____

☐ _____   ☐ _____

Summary of Meeting:

_____

_____

_____

_____

_____

_____

_____

_____

_____

Action Items:	**Person Responsible:**	**Due:**
_____	_____	_____
_____	_____	_____
_____	_____	_____
_____	_____	_____
_____	_____	_____

Agenda items for next meeting:	**Critique of this meeting:**
_____	_____
_____	_____
_____	_____
_____	_____

Appendix A:
A Problem-Solving Process

Appendix A: A Problem Solving Process

INTRODUCTION

It seems to be part of the nature of projects that they are riddled with problems. Much of a project leader's time will be spent working with team members to solve the problems that come up throughout the life of the project. In doing this, it is helpful to have some tools that will make the job easier.

Prior to getting into the model and the tools that support it, a discussion of problem-solving in general is appropriate.

THE APPROACH

For some reason western societies are, on the surface, much more action-driven than most other cultures. In the West, we like to "get things going." While this is an admirable quality under some circumstances, it is not always the best approach to solving problems. There is a tendency to "shoot from the hip" when confronted with a problem. The "Ready! Fire! Aim!" mentality was discussed briefly in an earlier chapter and bears repeating here.

The phrase, "just do it," that has become an advertising slogan for the fitness craze is also part of the thinking of most organizations. Other manifestations of this thought pattern are phrases like:

- "Don't just sit there. Do something!"

- "Anyone who can remain calm in the midst of all this chaos simply doesn't understand the situation."

- "Idle hands are the devil's playthings."

Our folklore is loaded with heroes who have triumphed over overwhelming odds. Most of these stories are about individuals who just "jumped in and did it." The stories don't tell anything about thinking through what needed to be done, planning how to best accomplish it and then methodically carrying out the plans.

The tendency to start acting without planning is not only less likely to actually solve the problem, it is also likely to be very expensive. False starts, having to backtrack and redo work, finding out after the designs are complete that the manufacturing process can't make the product, etc., are just some of the ways the "just do it" approach can cost in both time and money.

Using a structured problem-solving process serves two main functions:

1. It provides a framework for thinking about the problem, potential solutions, and effective implementation.

2. It provides a process by which ideas and alternatives can be examined and evaluated before much time or money is spent finding out which ones will work.

Having said that, it should be noted that the complete process, in all of its detail, is not necessarily appropriate for every problem encountered during a project. The process is not overly complex but it can be time-consuming, and time is something in short supply on most projects. There are, however, situations that demand a comprehensive approach to problem-solving. In these cases, the process should be followed carefully. One example of a good place to use the whole process is the Needs Analysis which should be conducted at the beginning of a project. In fact, the process itself is a model of how to plan and implement a project.

"As Is" and "To Be"   At the foundation of any problem-solving process is the problem statement and some idea of what a desirable solution would look like. According to this process, a good problem statement contains two specific parts:

The "As Is" portion of the statement contains a description of the situation exactly as it is — with no implication of why it is the way it is and with no indication of what should be done about it. This portion of the statement should be based on facts as much as possible. For example:

• Employees rate the food selection, quality and service in the company cafeteria at 2.3 on a scale of 1 to 5 (with 1 being lowest and 5 being highest) according to a survey conducted on March 1st of this year.

This statement simply states the facts according to the survey. There is no indication of why the employees don't think much of their cafeteria. There is no indication that, for instance, hiring more servers or offering a wider variety of food would solve the problem. In fact, from this statement, the solution (or solutions) are not at all clear.

The "To Be" portion of a good problem statement contains the desired outcome of solving the problem. It does not contain any indication of how the problem will be solved — only how we will know that it has been solved. For example:

• Employees will rate the overall food selection, quality and service in the company cafeteria at 4 or above when the March 1st survey is re-administered in July of this year.

There is no indication of how this improvement will be accomplished. This statement simply provides a statement of how to determine whether the problem was solved.

Working on a problem stated in this manner requires that the problem be analyzed to determine exactly why the "as is" situation exists and how the "To Be" condition can be achieved.

Defining problems using this method will go a long way toward preventing jumping into solutions without really looking at the problem.

THE PROCESS

This problem-solving process is a structured approach to the identification, analysis and solution of problems.

In Appendix B of this section are instructions for using a number of tools. Most of the tools are presented as worksheets that can be copied or used as models for working on various aspects of the problem-solving process. Others are described as processes that can be used in specific situations. Review them and test the tools that seem interesting or appropriate.

The process consists of six specific steps:

1. Stating the problem.

2. Analyzing the problem.

3. Generating potential solutions.

4. Selecting and planning the solution.

5. Implementing the solution.

6. Evaluating the solution.

Even though these steps are illustrated as sequential, problems rarely lend themselves to a single trip around the wheel. In many cases, it is necessary to back up and repeat one or more of the steps as new information becomes available.

Overall, the process is a logical progression of questions. The answers to the questions lead to the next step in the process. In steps one through four, there are brainstorming activities followed by evaluation and selection activities. In the brainstorming pieces, creativity and innovation are encouraged — the search for wide-ranging alternatives. In the evaluation and selection activities, the alternatives are examined and measured against criteria to determine which to pursue and which to discard.

Define the Problem   Every good problem-solving process begins with a clear definition of the problem to be addressed. This is the basis for all the work that follows. There are two pieces to a good problem statement:

- The "as is" portion of the statement describes the problem in objective, measurable terms. It should contain only those aspects of the problem that can be observed. It should not contain implications of either causes or solutions. In other words, it is a statement of "what," not "why" or "how."

Developing this objective statement can be more difficult than it appears on the surface. It is sometimes hard to keep the implication of cause and solution out of it.

- The second part of the statement is the "to be" portion in which the desired outcome of the problem-solving effort is stated. This also needs to be an objective statement of observable, measurable results. As with the "as is" portion, this part of the problem statement should not contain implications of either cause or solution.

Since what you are really doing in developing the problem statement is developing a goal for the problem-solving activity, consider using the goal development process described in Chapter 2: **Project Pre-Work**. Build the problem statement in pieces, using the Post-it® Note process. You can rearrange the parts in several ways and remove anything that implies cause and solution. The object is to achieve a statement that will guide the work of solving the problem.

Process   The process of developing the problem statement should encourage exploration of the situation in detail. Some of the questions you could use include:

- What do we see that tells us that something is wrong?

- How can we measure the difference between what we're seeing and what we think we should be seeing?

- What are the apparent parts of this problem?

- Is there a pattern to what we're seeing?

Various techniques can help with this initial evaluation. Flowcharting is a good one to use to get a good picture of how the problem situation works.

- Map the situation from beginning to end.

- Place a decision diamond after each identifiable step. The decision is a "Yes" or "No" answer to the question: "Is this correct?" or "Is this what we should expect?" When the answer is "No," examine that step further to determine what is wrong. The descriptions of what is wrong become part of the "as is" portion of the problem statement. The information about what should be becomes part of the "to be" portion.

- Develop a draft problem statement from the resulting information.

- Discuss the statement and refine it.

Another way to approach writing the problem statement is to have a group brainstorm about the situation.

- Let the brainstorming run freely until a number of possibilities have been advanced.

- Discuss each idea, clarifying the details and probing for additional information.

- Eliminate those pieces that are obviously not part of the problem and combine those that have distinct similarities.

- Develop one or more problem statements for the remaining items.

- Discuss the resulting problem statements and further refine them into a single "as is" and "to be" description of the problem.

Before moving on to the next step, be sure you can answer "Yes" to the following:

- Is the problem statement objective, stated in terms that only describe the observable facts and that do not imply either cause or solution?

- Is the "to be" portion of the statement also objective, stated in terms that describe what will be observable when completed and that do not imply either cause or solution?

- Is the problem sufficiently limited in scope or does the problem statement describe a series or group of problems that should be dealt with separately?

Tools Tools that can help with this step include:

- Brainstorming

- The Post-it® Goal Development Process

- Problem Selection Worksheet

- Weighted Voting

Analyze the Problem

With a clear, measurable problem statement, the scope and direction of analysis should be fairly obvious. One thing to remember in doing problem analysis is that, particularly when working with a group of people, graphic visual tools are very helpful. Use the tools that will allow you to display data visually. Cause and Effect Analysis, Why-Why Analysis, and Force Field Analysis are all examples of tools that lend themselves to this.

In analyzing the problem, the goal is to determine the root cause or causes of the problem. The symptoms of the problem are a clue to the root causes but they are not usually the actual root cause. Discovering the symptoms can lead to discovering the root cause. In a very simple example, the route to the root cause might look something like this:

- Problem: There is oil on the floor around the base of machine #3. This presents a safety hazard.

- Symptom: Oil is observed on the floor at the base of machine #3.

- Question: Why is there oil on the floor?

- Answer: Because there is a leak in the lubrication system of the machine.

It would be easy to stop at this point, fix the leak and get on with other things. However, the real question is: "Why did the leak develop?"

So, we follow the process a little further:

- Question: Why is there a leak in the lubrication system?

- Answer: Because a worn part was not replaced as scheduled.

- Question: Why wasn't the part replaced?

- Answer: Because, due to work load, scheduled preventative maintenance was not done.

We now find that the problem was preventable. In addition, we now know that preventative maintenance was not done as scheduled which, in turn, could lead us to look for other, potential, problems that could result from this lack of maintenance. Also, if we simply fix the existing leak and do nothing to ensure that preventative maintenance occurs as scheduled, we could see this same problem develop in other machines in the area.

Notice how each of the questions in the above example starts with the word "Why." This is the question that you need to answer in this step of the problem solving process. Asking the "Why" question several times can often lead to the root cause. (See: Why-Why Analysis in the Problem Solving Tools section.)

Another way to approach problem analysis is to use the Cause and Effect Analysis technique developed by Professor Kaoru Ishikawa. (See: Cause and Effect Analysis in the Problem Solving Tools section.)

Before moving on to the next step, be sure you can answer "Yes" to the following questions:

- Does the data we have collected confirm that the problem exists?

- Does the data we have collected support our description of the problem?

- Are the root causes of the problem, as we've defined them, supported by our analysis?

Tools Tools that can help with this step include:

- Cause and Effect Analysis

- Checksheets

- Force Field Analysis

- Point-Scoring Evaluation Form

- Paired Comparison Evaluation Form

- Why-Why Analysis

Generate Possible Solutions

Distrust the obvious. Don't jump to the conclusion that the first solution you come up with is the best solution.

With the data from the previous step in hand, turn your mind loose to see how many ways you can solve the problem. This is another excellent application for Brainstorming. At this point, however, limit the brainstorming activity to the generation of ideas. Save the analysis and evaluation for the next step.

The goal here is quantity — not necessarily quality. You are looking for as many ways as possible to solve the problem, including some that are pretty "off the wall." Even the most ridiculous idea may lead to the development of an idea that will actually work. Encourage people to "think outside the box" of their expertise and experience. This also means that you must maintain careful control over the brainstorming process to ensure that there is no evaluation or criticism of ideas as they are generated.

Process   Set up a classic brainstorming session. Have a flipchart, a white board, or other visible place to record ideas.

- Start the process by reviewing both the problem statement and the data from the analysis.

- Ask one or more of the following questions to get the process moving:

  - How can the causes of this problem, either individually or in groups, be eliminated?

  - How can we overcome this problem?

  - What can we do to ensure that this problem doesn't occur again?

  - What is the simplest and the most creative way you can think of to solve this problem?

- Record the resulting ideas as presented. Try to record the exact words used to state the idea. Discourage explanations and justifications. Encourage the free flow of ideas. If you can't write that fast, ask for a chance to catch up and then let the free flow pick up again.

- If the group gets stuck, refer to the Thought Provokers in the Problem Solving Tools section. This list can help break the blockage and stimulate some fresh thinking.

- When the list seems as complete as it is likely to get, ask for clarification. This activity is for clarification only — it should not be used to defend or promote specific ideas. Encourage people to state what they meant in clearer terms and to provide some specific information if that will help others understand the idea.

With few exceptions, this step and the first part of the next step; Select and Plan the Solution, are completed in the same working session. Just keep in mind that they are two distinct steps.

Before moving on the next step, be sure you can answer "Yes" to the following questions:

- Is this as complete a list of possible solutions as we can develop within a reasonable time?

- Have we been as creative as possible?

- Are the ideas clear?

Tools Tools that can help with this step include:

- Brainstorming

- Mind Mapping

- Thought Provokers

Select and Plan the Solution The first part of this step, the selection of the solution to be implemented, can follow the previous step immediately. The planning portion of this step may take longer than one working session depending on the complexity of the solution.

Process For the first part of this step, the selection process, try the following process:

- Have the group suggest, and list on a flipchart, white board, or other medium, criteria that could be used to evaluate alternative solutions.

- Discuss and select the criteria to be used.

- Apply the criteria to each proposed solution. Use both opinion-based methods such as Weighted Voting and more data-driven methods such as Alternative Rating Forms or Point Scoring Evaluation Forms as appropriate. The key is to apply the same process to every alternative.

- Remember that new solutions are likely to arise during this process. Do not discount them. Record them and run them through the same analysis process. These new alternatives frequently incorporate the best aspects of several other alternatives and may yield the best overall alternative.

- When agreement about which alternatives might best solve the problem seems close, consider using Force Field Analysis as a final test for a viable solution.

- Decide on the actual solution to be implemented.

The second part of this step, the planning of the implementation and measurement of the results, should follow the same basic process as project planning in general. The Post-it® Note process can be used for this planning if desired.

- Determine the major tasks to be accomplished and order them in sequence and in parallel.

- Add detail in the form of sub-tasks.

- Assign responsibilities and other levels of involvement for the individuals who will work on the implementation.

- Assign schedule estimates.

- Review the total plan for logical order and utilization of resources.

- Identify points where problems could occur and develop contingency plans.

- Determine how the effectiveness of the solution will be measured and develop whatever plans are necessary to carry out this evaluation.

- Document the plan.

Before moving on to the next step, be sure that you can answer "Yes" to the following questions:

- Have we worked through all the options and decided on the one most likely to actually solve the problem?

- Have we taken into account all the steps needed to implement the solution?

- Have we included the measurement criteria we will use to determine the effectiveness of the solution?

- Have we documented our plan?

Tools   Tools that can help with this step include:

- Alternative Rating Form

- Brainstorming

- How-How Analysis

- Paired Comparison Evaluation Form

- Point-Scoring Evaluation Form

- Post-it® Note Planning Process

- Solution Selection Worksheet

Implement the Solution   Here, also, the processes of project management in general apply. In this case, it is the Monitor, Measure, Problem-Solve, Report cycle of on-going project management.

Implementation of the solution should be treated as a separate project. It should be monitored and measured against its own criteria.

Process   Some things to keep in mind include:

- Monitor activities frequently. Keep yourself and the people working on the implementation informed about activities as often as necessary to ensure smooth implementation.

- Measure the work being done against the criteria developed for this purpose. When deviations occur, find out why and fix them if necessary.

- Be flexible. If reality says the plan is wrong, you have two choices: you can try to change reality or you can change the plan to reflect the real situation. Changing the plan is usually a lot easier than changing reality.

- Implement contingency plans as needed. Don't hope the problem will go away by itself. They rarely do.

- Communicate frequently and thoroughly with everyone impacted by the implementation.

Before moving on the next step, be sure you can answer "Yes" to the following questions:

- Have we followed our plan?

- Did we make the adjustments necessary along the way?

- Have we documented what we did?

- Are we ready to measure the effectiveness of our solution?

Tools   Tools that can help with this step include:

- The implementation plan

Evaluate the Solution   This is the piece that is missing from many problem-solving processes. Many of them stop at the implementation phase. What this fails to take into consideration is whether the problem has actually been solved, whether it will stay solved, and whether something else got broken in the process.

This evaluation "closes the loop" on the problem-solving process. Here is where you find out whether you have achieved your "to be" state as defined in the original problem statement. Without this evaluation, your problem-solving work is not done.

Process   Evaluation of the effectiveness of the solution should follow much the same process as a Post-Project Evaluation (See the Post-Project Evaluation Checklist in the Forms and Checklist section).

To gather the information to evaluate:

- Collect data according to the evaluation process developed as part of the plan.

- Compare this information against the "to be" state as defined in the problem statement.

- Compare it against the analysis of the problem from the second step of the process to verify that all the causes have been addressed.

- Verify that no new problems have resulted from the implementation.

Before leaving the problem-solving process, be sure you can answer "Yes" to the following questions:

- Have we solved the problem we set out to solve?

- Do we believe it will stay solved?

- Are we sure we haven't created any new problems in the process?

Tools   Tools that can help with this step include:

- The implementation plan.

- The evaluation criteria developed as part of the implementation plan.

- Post-Project Evaluation checklist.

CONCLUSION   This process is useful when there is enough time to actually complete the work involved in using it. Obviously, this process is time-consuming and data-intensive. It is not intended to be used on every little problem that comes up.

However, the concepts and the steps of the process — a step-by-step examination of the problem and its potential solutions — are valuable in virtually every problem situation.

The tools included in Appendix B can be used with or without the process, as the situation warrants.

Appendix B:
Problem-Solving Tools

Brainstorming

Description:

The purpose of brainstorming is to generate a large quantity of ideas from a group in a relatively short period of time. Brainstorming is best done in a small group.

Brainstorming is an idea-generating technique pioneered by Alex Osborn, an advertising executive. A group of people throw out their ideas as they think of them, so that each has the opportunity to build on the ideas of others.

Brainstorming is not a free-for-all. There is a discipline to the process that helps maintain both a sense of order and a reasonable level of freedom. The informality of the process is what generates the atmosphere of freedom. There are two phases to the brainstorming process: Idea-generation and idea-sorting and evaluation.

Directions, Phase 1:

The rules for the idea-generating phase of brainstorming are:

- No evaluation. Ideas must not be criticized or praised during the idea-generating phase.
- Encourage wild ideas. Some of the most off-the-wall ideas lead to practical solutions.
- Hitchhike. Build on the ideas of others.
- Strive for quantity. Quality comes later.

There are three basic methods of brainstorming. Each has its advantages and disadvantages. Each is described below.

Free-Wheeling Brainstorming
- Group members call out their ideas as they think of them.
- They are recorded, usually on a flip chart or white board, as fast as they are generated.
- An attempt is made to record the idea exactly as stated, using the contributor's exact words.

+	−
The advantages of the free-wheeling process are:	The disadvantages of the free-wheeling process are:
• It is very spontaneous — ideas come from all over, all at once.	• Strong individuals may dominate the session — everyone must be encouraged to participate.
• It tends to be very creative — if the "no criticism" rule is strictly observed, the ideas tend to be more creative as the process unfolds.	• It can be confusing, particularly for the person recording the ideas, when too many people talk at once. Ideas can get missed.
• It is easy to build on the ideas of others — because there is no need to wait, if an idea sparks a thought, it can be added to the list immediately.	

Round-Robin Brainstorming
- The group leader or the person recording the ideas, asks each person, in turn, for an idea — people need to wait for their turn to speak.
- Group members can pass on any round — if you don't have an idea, you pass.
- The session continues until everyone has passed during the round.
- Ideas are recorded in the same manner as in Free-Wheeling Brainstorming.

+	−
The advantages of the Round-Robin process are:	The disadvantages of the Round-Robin process are:
• It is difficult for one person to dominate the session since everyone gets a turn.	• It can be difficult to wait for one's turn to speak.
• The generation of ideas tends to be somewhat more focused.	• Due to the structured nature of the process, some loss of energy usually occurs.
• Everyone is encouraged to take part in the process.	• Some people will show a reluctance to pass. This can hold up the process while they try to think of something to contribute, further draining energy.
	• Because of the one-at-a-time approach, it is more difficult to build on the ideas of others.

Slip-Method Brainstorming
- This method is quite different from the previous two.
- The leader asks participants to write down ideas on small slips of paper, Post-it® Notes, or index cards.
- The cards are then collected and organized.
- Review of the submitted ideas can be by the group that generated them or by another group.

+	−
The advantages of the slip method are:	The disadvantages of the slip method are:
• The anonymous nature of the input can be used to deal with sensitive subjects.	• Due to the anonymous nature of the input, it is impossible to build on the ideas of others.
• This method can be very useful with large groups.	• The process is slow.
• The fact that no one need speak can be a relief for some people who are reluctant to speak in groups.	• Some ideas may be illegible or incomplete and hard to understand.
	• It is difficult to get clarification.

Phase 2

The second phase of brainstorming is the idea-sorting and evaluation phase. This needs to be a separate activity from the first phase. Do not get the two mixed up. Evaluation during the idea-generating process can be fatal to the creation of new ideas. Ideas are fragile things when they are fresh. They don't survive criticism very well. Let the generation phase run until the ideas begin to dry up, then move on to the sorting and evaluation phase.

Idea Sorting

This activity is intended to reduce the size of the list of ideas generated by grouping them logically together. After the group has stopped presenting new ideas, ask them to help with the sorting by identifying those ideas that seem to belong together. The groupings should be fairly obvious. Ideas that are similar in intent, content, wording, etc., should be grouped together. This can generate a whole new (but shorter) list. Try for agreement about how to word the explanation of the newly grouped ideas. This should result in more fully described ideas.

Idea Evaluation:

In this part of the exercise, the ideas are open for debate, criticism and evaluation. They can be examined for merit and debated for viability. The results of this process should be a list of ideas to be pursued and developed. The decision about which ideas to pursue should be a group decision.

Cause and Effect Diagrams

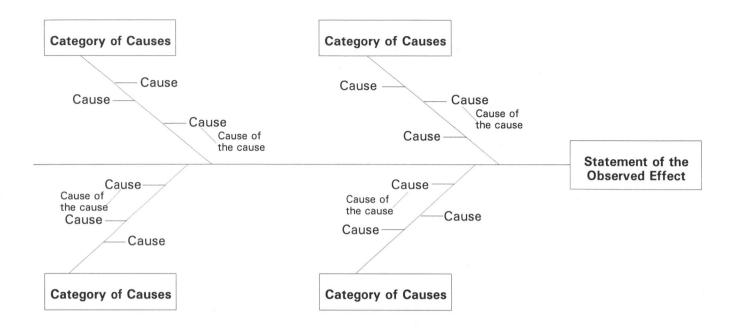

Description:

Cause and Effect Analysis is used to help structure the examination of a problem in order to determine the root cause of the problem rather than the symptoms. The process is useful on a wide variety of problem types.

General Directions:

Begin by drawing the basic Cause and Effect Diagram. This consists of the Effect box at the right, the center line, and branches to Categories of Causes. Determine the Categories. (As a starting point, the standard categories are Machines, Materials, Methods, Manpower, and sometimes Money.) Any categories that are appropriate to the problem can be used.

Standard Cause and Effect Directions:

Begin brainsotrming causes within each category. As causes are identified, it may become apparant that there are additional causes of the causes. These are branched from the initial cause. If a cause seems significant enough, it can become the effect in another analysis. Once causes have been identified, data can be collected to determine the extent and impact of each one.

Process-Analysis Cause and Effect Analysis Directions:

To look at a complete process using this technique, create a series of diagrams corresponding to the steps in the process. The "effect" of each diagram is the output of that process step. The "causes" of each "effect" are the process activities that create the output. Processes can be examined for efficiency, effectiveness, and problems created along the process.

Reverse Cause and Effect Analysis Directions:

Cause and Effect Analysis can also be used to determine the causes neede to create or drive a desired effect. For this analysis, place the desirec effect in the Effect Box, create the Categories of Causes and brainstorm the causes that will create the desired effect.

Checksheet

Description of the Event or Item to be Tracked	Time Periods during which data is to be collected (hours, days, weeks, etc.)										Totals
Totals											

Description:

There are two questions to be answered in order to set up a Checksheet:
1. What do we want to know?
2. What is the most reliable way to collect the data?
Information on Checksheets is usually collected in categories: by product, by production operation, by date, by work shift, etc. In constucting Checksheets try to form categories that will be easy for the person recording the data to use. The data recorder should not have to make difficult judgements about when and where to put information on the form.

Directions:

Prepare the blank Checksheet. List the time periods, during which data will be collected, across the top. List the data being collected down the left. (The occurance of defects is the most common data tracked.) The number of times a particular defect is discovered during each time period is indicated by a simple "hash mark" (/) in the appropraite box. Totals are developed both vertically and horizontally.

Cost-Benefit Analysis

Description:

Cost-Benefit Analysis is a tool for comparing the known cost and potential benefits of a proposed action. Some things are relatively easy to evaluate using Cost-Benefit Analysis even if it involves making some assumptions, (e.g., that the proposed solution will result in a 25% improvement in productivity) that will have to be verified after the implementation. If you can get agreement that the assumptions are valid, you should have little trouble getting your analysis accepted.

Some situations do not lend themselves to "hard numbers" analysis. In other words, the evaluation should be based on something other than cost and the dollar value of benefits. For these "softer" issues, it may be helpful to simply answer two questions: "What do I give?" and, "What do I get?" In all cases the approach is to find some measure, usually dollars, and estimate the costs and benefits associated with a given choice.

Directions:

Develop a list of the costs associated with the proposed action. This should include both "out-of-pocket" expenses such as purchase price and installation costs, etc. It should also include "hidden" costs such as production down-time during installation, operator retraining, etc.

Develop a list of the benefits associated with the proposed action. This should include such things as increased productivity, reductions in waste, faster turnaround, money saved, etc. This may involve making some assumptions about what those benefits will be. If so, be sure to gain agreement about your assumptions before proceeding.

Develop the analysis using a format similar to the one in the example below:

Example:

A group has decided to purchase a new piece of equipment in order to address a problem with excessive waste in a production operation. The equipment will cost $1,000.00.

Costs

Machine	$1,000
Rewiring and installation expense	500
Cost of operator retraining	250
Cost of lost production during installation	500
Total cost	**$2,250**

Benefits

Reduce rejects by 10% (assumption)	$ 750
Reduce personnel hours for the job (assumption)	500
Reduce set-up time (assumption)	250
Total benefits	**$1,500**

Comparing the costs and benefits over two years shows:

	Costs	Benefits	Profit
Year #1	$2,250	$1,500	($750)
Year #2	0	$1,500	$750
Totals	**$2,250**	**$3,000**	**$750**

In two years the new equipment will pay back the original cost and generate $750 in additional income.

Force Field Analysis — Worksheet

Force Field Analysis helps groups identify those forces within the organization that will help drive a desired change and those that will hinder the change. The "To Be" statement (the result of the change) is represented by the center line of the diagram. Forces are usually shown as arrows: The Driving forces are pushing toward the center while the Hindering forces are pushing against the center.

Some groups use a scale (e.g.: 1 = very weak to 5 = very strong) to evaluate the relative impact of the forces. For graphic representation, arrows of the length that represents their relative strength are used.

Example:

  As Is statement: _____

  To Be statement: _____

Forces that will help drive the change					Forces that will hinder the change				
5	4	3	2	1	1	2	3	4	5

Directions:

Draw a line down the center of a sheet of paper. This represents the "To Be" statement — what you want the situation to be when the change is complete. The group then identifies and lists the Driving forces to the left of the center line and the Hindering forces to the right of the center line.

Arrows are drawn which represent the perceived strength of each force. Once the diagram is complete, the group can use the information to generate potential ways of strenthening Driving forces and weakening Hindering forces.

Note: In most situations, the data developed in Force Field Analysis is primarily subjective (based on opinion rather than verifiable fact).

Force Field Analysis — Example

Force Field Analysis helps groups identify those forces within the organization that will help drive a desired change and those that will hinder the change. The "To Be" statement (the result of the change) is represented by the center line of the diagram. Forces are usually shown as arrows: The Driving forces are pushing toward the center while the Hindering forces are pushing against the center.

Some groups use a scale (e.g.: 1 = very weak to 5 = very strong) to evaluate the relative impact of the forces. For graphic representation, arrows of the length that represents their relative strength are used.

Example:

As Is statement: Morale, as identified in the latest Employee Opinion Survey, is low. Department employees rated morale at an average of 2 on a scale where 1 = low and 5 = high.

To Be statement: Department employees rate morale at or above 4 on the same scale when the same survey is retaken in three months.

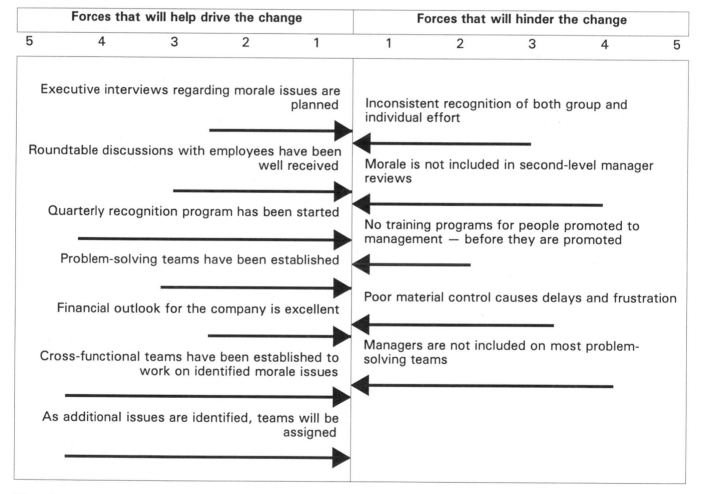

Forces that will help drive the change					Forces that will hinder the change				
5	4	3	2	1	1	2	3	4	5

Executive interviews regarding morale issues are planned

Roundtable discussions with employees have been well received

Quarterly recognition program has been started

Problem-solving teams have been established

Financial outlook for the company is excellent

Cross-functional teams have been established to work on identified morale issues

As additional issues are identified, teams will be assigned

Inconsistent recognition of both group and individual effort

Morale is not included in second-level manager reviews

No training programs for people promoted to management — before they are promoted

Poor material control causes delays and frustration

Managers are not included on most problem-solving teams

Directions:

Draw a line down the center of a sheet of paper. This represents the "To Be" statement — what you want the situation to be when the change is complete. The group then identifies and lists the Driving forces to the left of the center line and the Hindering forces to the right of the center line.

Arrows are drawn which represent the perceived strength of each force. Once the diagram is complete, the group can use the information to generate potential ways of strenthening Driving forces and weakening Hindering forces.

Note: In most situations, the data developed in Force Field Analysis is primarily subjective (based on opinion rather than verifiable fact).

How-How Analysis

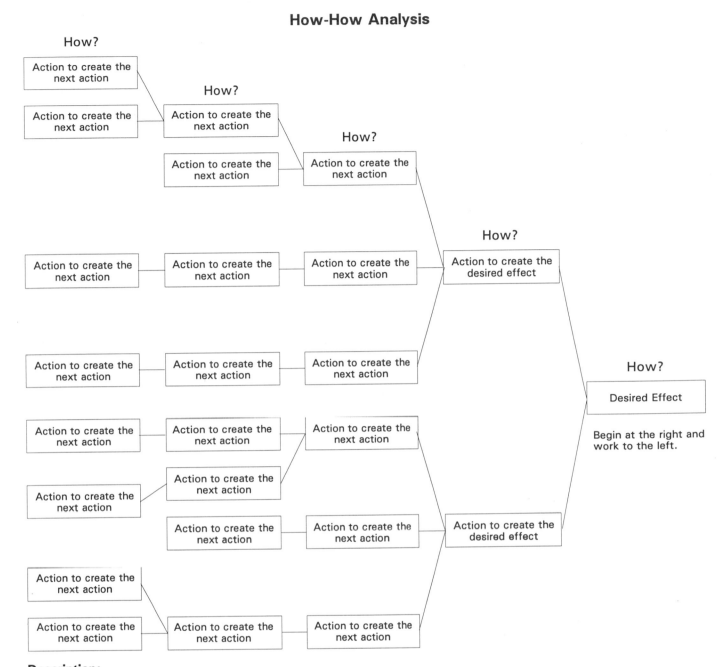

How? — Action to create the next action

How? — Action to create the next action

How? — Action to create the next action

How? — Action to create the desired effect

How? — Desired Effect

Begin at the right and work to the left.

Action to create the next action (repeated)

Action to create the desired effect

Description:

How-How Analysis is similar to the Cause and Effect Diagram in that both processes can be used to uncover the root causes of problem. They both begin with a specific situation that needs to be broken into causative elements. Unlike Cause and Effect Analysis (and its variation, Why-Why Analysis), How-How asks the how you can intentionally bring about the result in the future, not inquire as to how a past effect can be understood. It can be used to test the implementability of a proposed solution. In structure, it looks like a Why-Why Analysis diagram reversed and is frequently used to test solutions developed using the Why-Why technique.

Directions:

Begin by creating the first box of the diagram at the right side of the page (roughly in the middle vertically.) Place the "effect" (the desired result) in this box. Ask the question: "How?" This is the question at every stage of this process. "How can this be achieved? How can this be done?" Branch the most obvious answers into the next column to the left. Then, taking each answer in turn, ask the "How?" question again and branch those answers into the next column. This process can be extended as far as necessary to uncover the root cause of the problem. As a general rule, if you ask "How?" five times, you will most likely be at the lowest practical level of detail.

Paired Comparison Evaluation Form

Options	Comparisons						
	A vs B	A vs C	A vs D	B vs C	B vs D	C vs D	Totals
A							
B							
C							
D							

Description:

Like Weighted Voting, using Paired Comparisons will help a group to quantify the preferences of its members. Each option (e.g., a potential solution) is compared against every other option. Votes are recorded. They are totaled only when all possible comparisons have been made.

The power of Paired Comparisons comes from the choices it forces group members to make. Even when two alternatives seem equal, members must choose one or the other. Having to make difficult choices often leads people to see advantages (or disadvantages) they may otherwise overlook. The highest total on a Paired Comparison chart does not automatically become the group's decision. In working toward consensus, the group can focus on the two or three highest-scoring options.

Directions:

See the chart below to determine the number of comparisons required for a given number of options. Set up the necessary grid. In each comparison, each member has one, and only one, vote. He or she must decide which of the two alternatives in the pair is better. (The total number of votes cast must be equal to the number of members in the group.) Everyone must cast a vote in each comparison, even if neither choice is particularly appealing.

Number of Options	Number of Comparisons
2	1
3	3
4	6
5	10
6	15
7	21
8	28

Point-Scoring Evaluation Form

Criteria	Max. Points	Items or Options to be Evaluated				
Totals						

Description:

A Point-Scoring system is a variation on Alternative Rating. One-thousand (1,000) points are divided among criteria in accordance with their relative importance. The group then reviews and discusses the options, assigning a number of points, up to the maximum for that criteria. The totals help clarify the group's preferences.

Driections:

Determine and define the criteria to be used in the evaluation. Distribute 1,000 points among the criteria in proportion to their importance. Review all options with respect to the first criteria and decide, as a group, how many points to allocate to each option — from 0 to the maximum for that criteria. Continue with the second criteria, then the third, etc.

Problem Selection Worksheet

Problem Statements ->				
Control Low 1 2 3 4 5 High				
Importance Low 1 2 3 4 5 High				
Difficulty High 1 2 3 4 5 Low				
Time High 1 2 3 4 5 Low				
Return on Investment Low 1 2 3 4 5 High				
Resource Requierments High 1 2 3 4 5 Low				
Total Points				

Control: The extent to which the group can control the problem and can control the solution.

Importance: The seriousness or urgency of the problem.

Difficulty: A judgement about the relative difficulty of working through the problem to a solution.

Time: A judgement about the relative length of time it will take to resolve the problem.

Return on Investment: The expected payoff from implementing the solution.

Resource Requirements: The amount of resources required to solve the problem (people, time, money, equipment, etc.).

Directions:

In the boxes across the top, write statements describing the various problems the group is considering. Then rate each problem against the listed criteria by working across each row. The object is to have the group reach a consensus about the rating to give to each problem in turn, based on each criteria. The higher the total score, the greater the likelihood that the problem is appropriate for the group to undertake.

Special Note:

The scales for three criteria: "Difficulty," "Time," and "Resource Requirements" run from High to Low. This is the opposite of the other criteria because, in these cases, the lower the requirement, the better.

Solution Selection Worksheet

Solution Statements ->				
Control Low 1 2 3 4 5 High				
Appropriateness Low 1 2 3 4 5 High				
Resource Availability Low 1 2 3 4 5 High				
Time High 1 2 3 4 5 Low				
Return on Investment Low 1 2 3 4 5 High				
Acceptability Low 1 2 3 4 5 High				
Total Points				

Control: The extent to which implementation of the solution is within the control of the group.

Appropriateness: The degree to which the solution satisfies the requirements of solving the problem.

Resource Availability: The extent to which the resources are available to the group.

Time: A judgement about the relative length of time it will take to resolve the problem.

Return on Investment: The expected payoff from implementing the solution.

Acceptability: The degree to which the people (and organization) involved will accept the changes.

Directions:

In the boxes across the top, write statements describing the various solutions the group is considering. Then rate each problem against the listed criteria by working across each row. The object is to have the group reach a consensus about the rating to give to each solution in turn, based on each criteria. The higher the total score, the greater the likelihood that the solution can be effectively implemented.

Special Note:

The scales for the "Time" criteria runs from High to Low. This is the opposite of the other criteria because, a shorter time requirement is more desirable.

"T" Charts

+	−

Description:

"T" Charts, also known as Balance Sheets or Balance Charts, allow a group to identify and review the pros and cons of a variety of options. Like other tools for reaching consensus, T-Charts won't make the decision. They will, however, help organize information and facilitate discussion among group members. "T" Charts can be particularly useful during meeting critique as a quick way to capture positive and negative comments about the meeting process. "T" Charts look much like Force Field Analysis, but they are quite different in purpose. Force Field is used to contrast the "as is" situation with the "to be" state to determine what is helping and what is hindering movement toward the "to be" state. A "T" Chart is a quick way to document the pros and cons of one or more choices.

Directions:

Simply mark a large "T" on a flip chart or white board. Label the left side "+" (pros) and the right side "−" (cons). List the positives in the left-hand column and the negatives in the right-hand column. The group can then discuss the relative merits (or disadvantages) of the items in each column. (An example of "T" Charts can be found in the description of Brainstorming in this Problem-Solving Tools section.)

Thought-Provokers

When faced with a problem, consider the questions on this list to help stimulate your thinking along alternative lines. Creativity is more a matter of looking at a problem from a slightly different angle than looking at it from a completely different direction.

Put it to other uses?
- A new way to use it as is?
- Other uses for it if modified?

Adapt it?
- What else is like this?
- What else does this suggest?
- Does the past offer a parallel?
- What could I copy?
- Whom could I emulate?

Modify it?
- Is there a new twist I could put on this?
- Could I change the meaning, color, motion, sound, odor, form, shape, etc.?
- Are there other changes I could make?

Magnify it?
- What could I add to this?
- Would more time make a difference?
- Would greater frequency make a difference?
- Could it be stronger?
- Could it be larger?
- Could it be higher?
- Could it be longer?
- Could it be thicker?
- Could I add extra value?
- What ingredient(s) could I add?
- Could I duplicate it?
- Could I multiply it?
- Could I exaggerate it?

Minimize it?
- What could I subtract from this?
- Could I make it smaller?
- Could it be condensed?
- How about a miniature version?
- Could it be lower?
- Could it be shorter?
- Could it be lighter?
- Could I omit something?
- Can it be streamlined?
- Can it be split up?
- Can it be understated?

Substitute something?
- Who else could do it?
- What else could be used instead?
- Can I use some other ingredient?
- Can I use some other material?
- Can I use some other process?
- Can it be some other place?
- Can it be some other time?
- Can it use some other form of power?
- Is there some other approach?
- Can I use some other tone of voice?

Rearrange it?
- Can I interchange components?
- Can I use another pattern?
- Can I use another layout?
- Would it work in some other sequence?
- Can I transpose the cause and effect?
- Can I change the pace?
- Can I change the schedule?

Reverse it?
- Can I transpose the positive and negative?
- How about opposites?
- Can I turn it backward?
- Can I turn it upside down?
- Can I turn it inside out?
- Can I reverse roles?
- Change shoes?
- Turn tables?
- Turn the other cheek?

Combine it?
- How about a blend, an alloy, an assortment, an ensemble?
- Can I combine units?
- Can I combine the purpose with another?
- Can I combine the appeal with another?
- Can I combine the ideas with others?

Weighted Voting Form

Individuals	Options				

Description:

Weighted Voting is a way to quantify the positions of group members. It differs from Criteria Rating in two ways. First, no decision criteria are used. Second, individual members' votes are recorded; there is no discussion or attempt to reach agreement on a single number. Once the voting is completed, the group can discuss the relative positions of various members and attempt to reach consensus.

Directions:

List the options being considered across the top. List individual group members down the left. Assign the number of votes each member will have to distribute among all options. (As a rule of thumb, the number of votes should be approximately 1-1/2 times the number of options.) Ask members, in turn, to distribute their votes among the options. Members may assign all their votes to one option or distribute them among several.

Why-Why Analysis

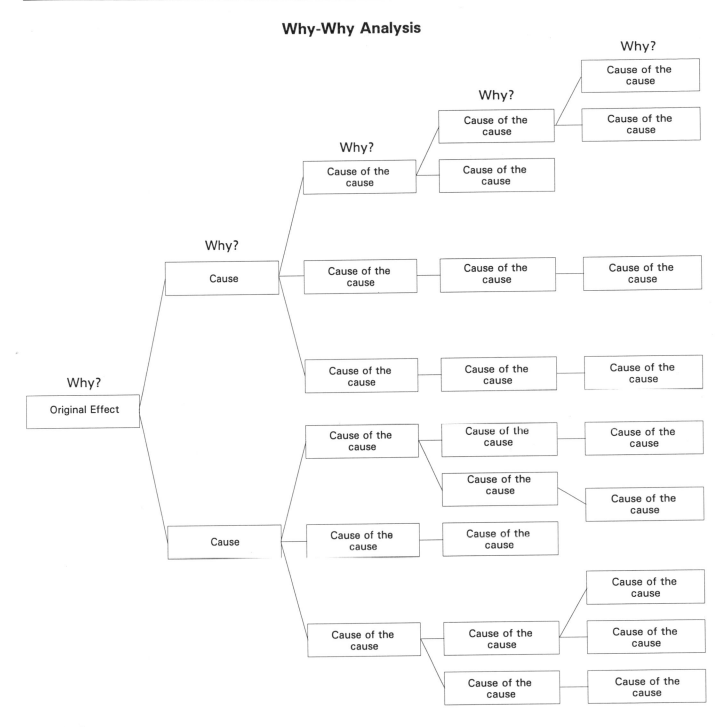

Description:

Why-Why Analysis is a variation of the Cause and Effect Diagram. Like Cause and Effect Analysis, it can be used to uncover the root causes of a problem. Also, like Cause and Effect Analysis, the process can be reversed (See: How-How Analysis) to develop the steps needed to achieve a desired effect.

Directions:

Begin by creating the first box of the diagram at the left side of the page (roughly in the middle vertically.) Place the "effect" (the observable condition) in this box. Ask the question: "Why?" This is the question at every stage of this process. "Why is this happening? Why is this the case?" Branch the most obvious answers into the next column to the right. Then, taking each answer in turn, ask the "Why?" question again and branch those answers into the next column. This process can be extended as far as necessary to uncover the root cause of the problem. As a general rule, if you ask "Why?" five times, you will most likely reach the root cause of the situation.

Attend a workshop based on this book!
Applying Project Management in the Workplace
"The Workshop"

Bring this innovative approach to Project Management into your organization. Jeff Crow, the author of Applying Project Management in the Workplace, provides customized workshops presenting the methodology, tools and techniques in this book. His workshops are highly interactive, involving participants in hands-on experience with the project management process.

✳ Customized Presentation

Workshops are customized to meet specific organizational needs and practices. Actual projects from the organization are used for the in-class exercises — not "canned" simulations. Participants not only experience the training, they also produce valuable work output in the process.

✳ The Workshop Experience

During these workshops, participants experience the total project management process, including:

* Working through the complete project definition process; defining needs and wants; determining constraints; identifying customers and stakeholders; developing project goals; and, identifying the skills needed to complete the project.
* Planning the project; defining major project phases; identifying, organizing, and sub-dividing tasks; establishing responsibilities; developing schedules; and, planning for contingencies.
* Simulating the implementation of the project; monitoring activities; managing information; problem-solving; updating status; managing changes; and, documenting activities.
* Simulating delivery of the final output; developing the final report; closing out the project; and, conducting a post-project evaluation.
* Applying many of the checklists, forms and tools.

✳ Multiple Projects, Multiple Experiences

To make the experience as meaningful and participative as possible, multiple projects are developed. In most workshops, three to five projects are worked on simultaneously. Brief presentations by each working group throughout the workshop give participants the benefit of their own experience as well as the experience of others. Over half of the workshop is hands-on work in small groups.

✳Other Workshops✳

In addition to **Applying Project Management in the Workplace**, workshops are also available on:
Work-Process Analysis and Re-design
Team Development
Team Building

For information, contact: **Crow Development Corporation**
PO Box 80746
Portland, OR 97280-1746
(503) 244-8486
Fax: (503) 977-7894
World Wide Web: www.crowdevelopment.com
E-Mail: jcrow@crowdevelopment.com